GET OUT OF TOWN!

BY
MATT HARDING
&
FREDDIE SNALAM

Published by
All Points Publishing, Inc.

First Edition Copyright ©1994 All Points Publishing, Inc.
PO Box 4832, Boulder, CO. 80306 USA

ISBN 1-884294-00-6

Printed in the United States of America

10 9 8 7 6 5 4 3 2 1

Contents

Golf

WARNING - DISCLAIMER

Hiking the Mesa Trail

FOREWORD

Boulder is without a doubt one of the premier sports towns in the USA, if not the world. Blessed with the mountains to the west and the high plains to the east, the town has something to offer just about every outdoor sports person - except perhaps the surfer and deep sea fisherman! Boulder's climate is renowned for its clear air and beneficial climate, which attracts athletes from around the world.

This book came about because we felt there was a need for a guide that covered a wide range of sporting activities in the locality. It is not intended to be totally comprehensive by subject. Other authors have done a better job at covering their own specialities. We have aimed to choose a selection of the best hikes, climbs, mountain bike rides etc. If you enjoy what you have found here, then the more detailed guides will undoubtedly assist you further. We have listed some of these guides, sorted by subject, in Reference 4.

The eagle-eyed will notice very quickly that there appears to be a gaping geographic hole in our research - namely the Rocky Mountain National Park. There is however a good reason for this. Due to its size and complexity, the Park offers enough material to justify a book of its own. For this reason, we have not covered it in this volume.

OUTFITTERS & SCHOOLS

For those activities such as ballooning or gliding, where it is not possible, or desirable, for the layman to do it himself, we have aimed to give an idea of what is available. In Reference 3, we have listed some of these schools, together with a contact telephone number. We cannot vouch for their suitability or competency in any way, and in addition, we have not received any support or advertising from them in exchange for inclusion in this book. It is for the individual customer to assess their competency before making any commitment.

WEATHER

Generally the weather in Boulder is ideally suited to the outdoor lifestyle. Summers tend to be long and warm, rarely too hot, and winters tend to alternate between cold snowy periods and warm sunny days. The much used local saying "If you don't like the weather, stick around because it will change in a moment" is not too far from the truth. Rarely does it do anything inconvenient like rain or snow for very long.

TIME REQUIRED

For activities where we have listed trails, such as hiking and mountain biking, we have given an estimated time required. This is only intended as a very rough guide. They translate as:

Full Day	5 - 8 hours
Half Day	2 - 5 hours
Not a lot	Less than 2 hours

MAPS & DIAGRAMS

We have deliberately avoided using excerpts of US Geological Survey maps to illustrate the trails because we find in general that the relevant section usually omits other information, such as where the route starts in relation to major highways and towns. We have endeavored to produce unique maps and drawings which, when used in conjunction with the text, should provide all the information you need. However, a good map is always handy to have on a trip, and one of the clearest we have found, is the Mountain Bike Map produced by Latitude 40°.

MAP SYMBOLS

-‒⁀‒-‒-	Main trail	~~~~	Creek
···········	Other Trails	~~⌐ ⌐~	Bridge
————	Road	▪▪ ▪ ▪▪	Buildings
+++++++++	Railroad	△	Campground
T	Trailhead & Parking	P	Additional Parking

Acknowledgements

As is usual with a project of this size, numerous people have helped with ideas, photos and justified criticism. We would like to thank the following who have provided valuable assistance: Lycia Adams, Pat Albright, Eric Bader, Brett Bartelson, Todd Bibler, John Coulton, Charlie Craven, Crusher, Steve Dorala, Dick DuMais, David Felkley, Ed Goss, Mark Grylicki, Jesse Guthrie, Phil Huff, Jay Johnson, Duncan Jones, Tony King, Alice Price Knight, Anne Krause, David Levin, Rob Linde & The Eldora Mountain Resort, Bruce Miller, Linda Rathbun, Bill Reef, Mark Rolofson, Scuba Joe, Jonathan B. Smith, Clyde Soles, Taz Vaughn, the gang at Velo News, Beth Wald, Scott Westfall, Dave Whaley, Jennifer Whaley and Michelle Zemko.

Don Cleary for his amazing balloon sculptures and zany humour.

And our Editors - Mark Springett & Wendy Sollod.

Finally, a special thank you must go to Babette Harding for keeping the Authors in line when the urge to drop everything and go climbing became almost too strong.

Front Range Geology

By Mark Springett

Boulder is uniquely situated where the plains and the Rocky Mountains meet. The plains continue eastwards from Boulder for some thousand miles, dropping gently in elevation from Boulder s 5,430 feet above sea level to less than a thousand feet; whereas turning westward the Front Range soars to some 8,000 feet in less than two miles and reaches altitudes of more than 13,000 feet at the Continental Divide, less than twenty miles west of the city center.

The diverse geology of the area provides the raw material for many of the activities described in other chapters; and an inherent appreciation of many geologic features and characteristics is a subconscious part of the rock-climbers skill or the kayakers interpretation of the white water ahead. The rocks of the area and the spectacular landforms that result from their juxtaposition, tell the history of the district as well as influencing the economic development of the area and even the weather that we experience.

A walk up Eldorado Canyon is a good way of developing an understanding of the role of the different geologic components of the terrain that forms the basis for our games. To the right is the creek with its water constantly carrying a load of sediments eroded from the rocks higher up the canyon, en route to the Gulf of Mexico. Behind, the plains stretch eastward with a certain monotony, interrupted close to the Front Range by occasional intrusions of basalt and dolerite. These intrusions represent the Tertiary turmoil resulting from the collision between the plains and the mountains creating such features as the Valmont Dyke, or further south at Golden, Table Mountain. Here, the basic volcanic rocks that were fed through fissures reached surface and spread out as lava flows, similar to those seen being created today in Hawaii or Iceland. These volcanic rocks were intruded through the underlying sedimentary rocks and the Cretaceous Pierre Shale, the youngest of the rocks that form the plains in the area around Boulder, apart from the very recent veneers of gravel, sand and clay that are today s erosional and depositional product. The view eastward from Eldorado is, to many, uninteresting and the eye naturally turns upwards and westward; where the cliffs soar, separated by ravines full of talus, the debris of erosion.

The Fountain Formation, the rock unit on which the Flatirons and most of the good climbing at Eldorado Canyon occurs, is some 270 million years old and is formed by the erosion of an earlier Rocky Mountain range. The red sandstones and quartz pebble conglomerates, with occasional finer grained layers, that we walk by or climb on, consist of eroded sands and gravels from the granites and gneisses that were formed 1.7 billion years ago. There are many locations where localized conglomerates with big, rounded quartz pebbles can be seen - for example on the Third Flatiron or at the foot of the Bastille in Eldorado Canyon. These conglomerates are testimony to torrential floods descending from the ancestral Rockies over very brief periods of time which may have been as brief as a day or so (just as the Big Thompson Canyon flood occurred in 1976). The roughness of the sandstones and conglomerates of the Fountain Formation add to their attractiveness as a medium on which to climb. The mineral constituents of the sandstones basically reflect their parentage, the granites of the Rockies, made up of three key minerals: quartz, feldspar and mica. Quartz and feldspar are both relatively hard and constitute most of the make-up of the Fountain Formation.

The Boulder Creek granite, dated at 1.7 billion years, that also provides an important part of the local rock climbing resource, is made up of these three key minerals, and has the same pleasant frictional characteristics as the Fountain Formation due to the mineralogic similarities. However granite weathers differently and the types of cracks that develop in granite differ from those in sandstone. Someone accustomed to climbing at Eldorado may be rudely surprised at the different feel of a hold on a similar class climb in Boulder Canyon.

Rocks younger than the Fountain Formation, but older than the Pierre Shale, are the Lyons Sandstone which is a very attractive building stone quarried at Lyons, north of Boulder, and has been used extensively in the construction of buildings at the University of Colorado. As the erosion of the ancestral Rockies continued, a shallow sea developed in the area and the Lykins formation, consisting of maroon shales was deposited, over this the Entrada sandstone was deposited representing a reversion to a more arid climate. This was succeeded by a more extensive development of coastal swamps and littoral settings where dinosaurs and tropical plants thrived. The Morrison Formation is rich in dinosaur footprints and the fossil leaves of tropical plants. The hogback ridge north of Morrison is very accessible and as this a good location for both bouldering and for seeking fossil plants, both these activities can be pleasantly combined.

Some 135 million years ago a large sea began to form in the area. The sands of the beaches were to become the Dakota sandstone and over this the Benton and Niobrara Formations were deposited. The next layer was the Pierre Shale which is well exposed in the small road cuts on US 36 between Boulder and Lyons as well as on the flanks of the Valmont Dyke where it has been baked by the heat of the basaltic lava.

Seventy million years ago the Laramide Orogeny, or mountain building period, caused the old granites and gneisses of the ancestral Rockies to rise again, eventually creating the Rocky Mountains that we know today. This upward thrust caused the adjacent sediments, from the Fountain Formation to the Pierre Shales to be tilted upward against the rising older rocks. These tilted formations, where they are formed of harder rocks make the distinctive hogback ridges culminating to the west in the Flatirons. During this period relatively small plugs of coarse-grained igneous rocks were intruded into the older granites and gneisses. Associated with these intrusives were a major series of mineralizing events which created the Colorado Mineral Belt

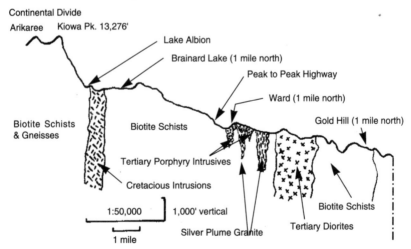

which trends southwestward from Jamestown through Idaho Springs and Leadville to the San Juan Mountains. In the Boulder area there are many veins that were mined underground for gold, tungsten, lead and silver and which triggered the initial economic development of the area. Old mine shafts and tunnels are prone to hazards from collapse and poisonous gases. These should be avoided.

Generalised Geological cross-section of the Boulder Area
West - East, just north of the city of Boulder

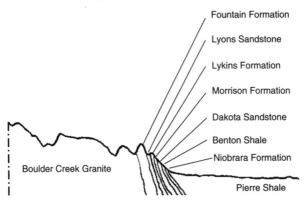

Fountain Formation

Lyons Sandstone

Lykins Formation

Morrison Formation

Dakota Sandstone

Benton Shale

Niobrara Formation

Boulder Creek Granite

Pierre Shale

Up, up and away, over East Boulder

Ballooning

Ballooning has been prominent in this area since around 1980, and increasingly more so in the last five years. In the Boulder area there are several companies providing tours.

Customarily balloon tours leave at sunrise, due to calmer air conditions early in the morning, with a minimum flight time of at least an hour. Distances covered average 5-20 miles depending upon wind speeds. A safe flying wind speed for tours is considered to be up to 10 miles per hour, so ballooning is a peaceful sport.

Apart from the thrill of being in a balloon, many choose to combine this with a champagne breakfast, and some even go all the way and get married in one! Whilst you may not want to go overboard with the romance of the situation, lighter than air flight is a unique experience and should not be missed. For a list of tour operators, see Reference 3.

There are at least a dozen dedicated recreational balloonists in the Boulder area. The typical cost of a hot air balloon is similar to an automobile - $20,000 will buy you a reasonable balloon, and under $10,000 will get a good used balloon. For a really fancy model with lots of gadgets, $30,000-$40,000 may be necessary.

Balloons vary in size with an average height of about 7 stories, with volumes anywhere from 75,000-200,000 cu. ft. The gas used to heat the air that fills the balloon is propane - same as a patio barbecue grill. The balloons have precise vertical control but are at the mercy of the winds for direction.

Balloons, and especially their pilots, are regulated and licensed by the FAA (Federal Aviation Authority) and must follow the same set of rules that govern all aviation.

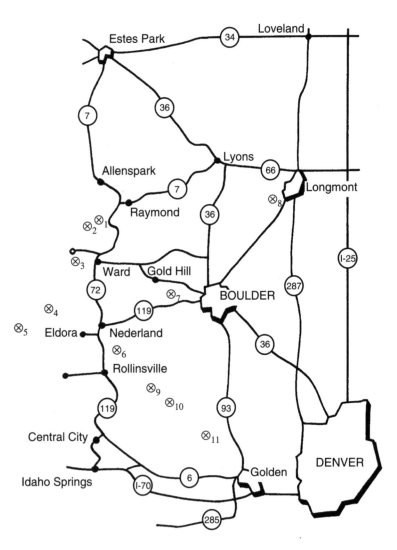

1: Peaceful Valley
2: Camp Dick
3: Pawnee Pass
4: Rainbow Lakes
5: Buckingham Campground
6: Kelly-Dahl

7: Boulder Mountain Lodge
8: Boulder County Fairgrounds
9: Reverend's Ridge
10: Aspen Meadows
11: White Ranch Park

Camping

Despite Boulders close proximity to large recreational areas, there are few campgrounds close to the town, and only one within walking distance. The US Forest Service maintains several on the edge of the Indian Peaks Wilderness Area which are very good, but they tend to be very busy during peak periods.

The Golden Gate Canyon State Park has two large campgrounds to offer, as well as a network of backcountry sites accessible only by foot, bicycle, or horse. These sites do not seem to get used as much as they deserve. You do need to carry in drinking water.

White Ranch, near Golden, also has a few backcountry sites available.

We feel that a quiet night spent at one of these relatively isolated sites - most are only a one hour walk from the road - is a great antidote to the stresses of modern life. If you are looking for a short break, we don't think you can beat packing a small tent, stove and a few necessities and heading out for one of these sites. Even though you may be only a few miles from 'civilization' it will feel like another world. Add to that the good prospect of seeing some interesting wildlife early the next morning makes this a cheap deal. With the backcountry sites in particular, but all sites in general, do make sure you pack out everything you pack in.

In these listings we have indicated where RV electrical hookup is possible. Some sites may only be accessible by rough roads and, for this reason, may not suit larger vehicles.

A final point about water. All surface water should be treated before being used, as it may be unfit for human consumption.

Peaceful Valley

Run by: US Forest Service	**# of sites:** 15
Open dates: 5/1 - 10/31	**Fee:** $6
Limit of stay: 14 nights	**Reservations:** Y
RV's: Y	
Drinking water: Y	**Fireplaces:** Y
Tables: Y	**Toilets:** Y

Directions: From Nederland, take the Peak to Peak Highway - Hwy. 72 - north for 6 miles to Peaceful Valley. Take a left and the campground is a short distance on the right.

Information: Campground is very popular. Reservations, particularly at weekends and during the summer months, are strongly recommended.

Camp Dick

Run by: US Forest Service	**# of sites:** 34
Open dates: 5/1 - 10/31	**Fee:** $6
Limit of stay: 14 nights	**Reservations:** Y
RV's: Y	
Drinking water: Y	**Fireplaces:** Y
Tables: Y	**Toilets:** Y

Directions: From Nederland, take the Peak to Peak Highway - Hwy. 72 - north for 6 miles to Peaceful Valley. Take a left and the campground is located 1 mile west.

Information: Campground is very popular. Reservations, particularly at weekends and during the summer months, are strongly recommended.

Pawnee Pass

Run by: US Forest Service	**# of sites:** 55
Open dates: 7/1 - 10/15	**Fee:** $6
Limit of stay: 14 nights	**Reservations:** Y
RV's: Y	
Drinking water: Y	**Fireplaces:** Y
Tables: Y	**Toilets:** Y

Directions: From Nederland, take Peak to Peak Highway - Hwy. 72 -

to Ward. At Ward take the Brainard Lake road west for 5 miles. The campground is on the left, just before Brainard Lake.

Information: Campground is very popular. Reservations, particularly at weekends and during the summer months, are strongly recommended.

Rainbow Lakes

Run by: US Forest Service   **# of sites:** 18
Open dates: See below   **Fee:** $0
Limit of stay: 14 nights   **Reservations:** N
RV's: N
Drinking water: N   **Fireplaces:** Y
Tables: Y   **Toilets:** Y

Directions: From Nederland, take the Peak to Peak Highway - Hwy. 72 - north for 7 miles. At a junction - sign for University of Colorado Mountain Research Station, take the Rainbow Lakes Road. Follow this road, past a turn right for the Research Station, and continue to its end. The campground is about 5½ miles from the junction with Hwy. 72.

Information: The access road is rough, although passable by most cars, with care. For information on whether the road is clear of snow and passable, call the US Forest Service (303) 444-6600. Be warned - there is no drinking water at this site.

Buckingham

Run by: City of Boulder Parks   **# of sites:** 10
Open dates: 7/1 - 10/15   **Fee:** $0
Limit of stay: 14 nights   **Reservations:** N
RV's: N
Drinking water: N   **Fireplaces:** N
Tables: Y   **Toilets:** Y

Directions: From Nederland, head south out of town and then take CR. 130 to the town of Eldora. Drive through the town, heading west. The road soon becomes a jeep trail. A junction is met after about a mile. Keep right and continue on. The campground is about 5 miles west of Eldora.

Information: Heavily used at weekends and during summer months. The access road is rough, but accessible to most cars. Parking is limited. Also known as Fourth of July Campground. Drinking water is not available at this site, although there is a stream. Call Boulder Mountain Parks for details. (303) 441-3408

Kelly-Dahl

Run by: US Forest Service   **# of sites:** 46
Open dates: 5/1 - 10/31   **Fee:** $6
Limit of stay: 14 nights   **Reservations:** Y
RV's: Y
Drinking water: Y   **Fireplaces:** Y
Tables: Y   **Toilets:** Y

Directions: From Nederland, take Highway 72 south. Where Hwy. 72 breaks left and goes down to Wondervu, continue towards Central City on Hwy.119. After another ½ mile, the campground is on the left.

Information: Campground is very popular. Reservations, particularly at weekends and during the summer months are strongly recommended.

Boulder Mountain Lodge

Run by: Privately owned.   **# of sites:** 25
Open dates: Year round   **Fee:** $14
Limit of stay: 14 nights   **Reservations:** N
RV's: Y
Drinking water: Y   **Fireplaces:** Y
Tables: Y   **Toilets:** Y

Directions: Located at entrance to Four Mile Canyon Drive, 2 miles out of Boulder up Boulder Canyon, Hwy. 119.

Information: Tel: (303) 444-0882
Motel accommodation is also available. Full service, showers and electrical hookup.

Boulder County Fairgrounds

Run by: Privately owned.   **# of sites:** 92
Open dates: Year round.   **Fee:** $10 - $13
Limit of stay: 14 nights   **Reservations:** Y

RV's: Y

Drinking water: Y   **Fireplaces:** N

Tables: Y   **Toilets:** Y

Directions: Take Diagonal Highway east from Boulder towards Longmont. The Fairgrounds Campsite is located at intersection of Hover & Nelson on the edge of town.

Information: Tel: (303) 678-1525.
Campground has full service, electrical hookup and showers.

Golden Gate Canyon State Park

Address: 3873 Hwy 46, Golden, CO. 80403

Tel: (303) 592-1502

Park Visitor Center is located at the south east entrance to the park and is open year-round.

Fees for camping are in addition to Park Entrance Fee.

Reservations can be made for campgrounds by calling - 470-1144 in Denver. (1-800-678-2267 outside of Denver). Reservations can be made a minimum of 3 days and maximum of 90 days in advance. There is a reservation fee of $6.75 per booking.

The Park also has 4 primitive back country shelters available. They have three sides and a roof with accommodation for up to six people. There are also 23 back country camping sites for tents. Back country permits must be obtained from the Visitor Center before use.

Reverends Ridge

Run by: Golden Gate Canyon State Park   **# of sites:** 106

Open dates: Year round.   **Fee:** $7

Limit of stay: 14 nights   **Reservations:** Y

RV's: Y (no hookups)

Drinking water: Y   **Fireplaces:** Y

Tables: Y   **Toilets:** Y

Directions: Reverend's Ridge Campground is situated in the north-west corner of the park.

Information: Showers available.

Aspen Meadows

Run by: Golden Gate Canyon State Park   **# of sites:** 35

Open dates: Year round.   **Fee:** $6

Limit of stay: 14 nights   **Reservations:** Y

RV's: N

Drinking water: Y   **Fireplaces:** Y

Tables: Y   **Toilets:** Y

Directions: The Aspen Meadows Campground lies in the northern section of the park.

Information: Tents only.

White Ranch Park

Administration Address: Jefferson County Open Space
                           700 Jefferson County Parkway, Suite 100,
                           Golden, CO. 80403
                           Tel: (303) 271-5925

The Park has a number of backcountry camp areas which are available by advance permit only. These can be picked up from the Open Space Office at the above address during office hours Monday through Friday.

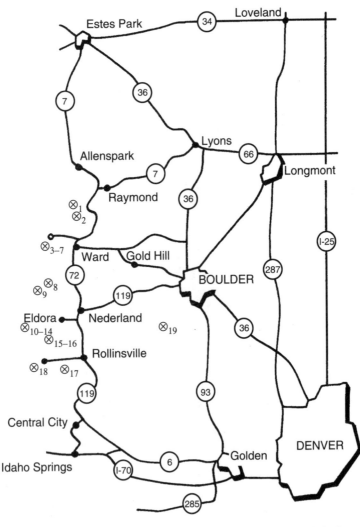

1.	Middle St. Vrain Valley	11.	Devils Thumb Lake
2.	Coney Flats	12.	King Lake
3.	Left Hand Park Reservoir	13.	Lost Lake
4.	Little Raven	14.	Fourth of July
5.	CMC South	15.	Jenny Creek
6.	Jean Lunning Scenic Trail	16.	Guinn Mountain
7.	Sourdough Trail - North	17.	Jenny Lind Gulch
8.	Sourdough Trail - South	18.	Forest Lakes
9.	Niwot Ridge	19.	Meyers Homestead
10.	Woodland Lake		

Cross-Country Skiing

The beauty of the Rocky Mountains in winter is well known. Perhaps less well known is the ease with which the mountains can be accessed during winter on cross-country skis. The continued growth of downhill skiing, especially in Colorado, and the seemingly annual increases in lift ticket prices, must be contributing factors to the popularity of cross-country skiing. Downhillers are spilling over into the woods as an alternative to crowded ski slopes. Let's hope the woods remain fairly tranquil! For about six months of the year it is possible to ski on trails in the forests, woods and open space around Boulder. For many Boulderites, the sport takes the place of hiking after the snow falls.

Far from being an elitist sport, cross-country skiing is become more mainstream and provides a marvellous way of getting about. Avoid the crowded I-70 and try the region around the Peak to Peak Highway. These trails can be almost eerily quiet, especially on weekdays. There are few experiences that can compare to a day out in the mountains when the weather is crystal clear and cold. Equally, the mountains can be extremely unwelcoming in bad weather, and you are advised to pay attention to weather reports before setting out.

For information on conditions try the local US Forest Service number (303) 444-6600.

The Forest Service has blazed some of the trails in this section with blue diamonds nailed to trees at irregular intervals. However, whilst these provide a useful service, it is unwise to rely entirely on them, particularly during bad weather.

Middle St. Vrain Valley

Distance: 5 miles one way
Difficulty: Moderate
Time required: Half day
Blue Diamond Blazed: Yes
Start Elevation: 8,520'   **Elevation Gain:** 1,080'

     A pleasant trip, offering a gradual ascent, excellent mountain views and mostly downhill on the return journey.

     Starts just west of Peaceful Valley at a bridge over Middle St. Vrain Creek. Peaceful Valley is 6 miles north of Ward on Hwy. 72.

     Ski out west from the Peaceful Valley trailhead, crossing the road bridge onto the north side of the valley. After one mile the trail crosses back over the Middle St. Vrain road and creek. Climb steadily through the trees, then down into the valley to end at the junction with the same road. Snowmobilers are often encountered on this trail so exercise caution.

     See trail map on the following page.

Sawtooth Mountain 12,304' - as seen from the Middle St. Vrain Valley

Coney Flats

Distance:	3 miles one way
Difficulty:	Moderate
Time required:	Half day
Blue Diamond Blazed:	No

Start Elevation: 9,190' **Elevation Gain:** 630'

A much-used trail within the Indian Peaks Wilderness.

Starts from Beaver Reservoir North Trailhead. From Nederland, drive north on Hwy. 72 towards Ward. Continue past Ward for a further 2½ miles to a left turn to Beaver Reservoir and Tahosa Camp (CR. 96). Follow CR.96 for another 2½ miles to the trailhead.

The trail heads west from the trailhead following a distinct trail to an exposed area - Coney Bench (also called Coney Flats). Avoid two left forks, the first a jeep track, the second the Beaver Creek Trail. The final section of the trail descends to the Middle St Vrain Road. Either turn around and return before the descent, or ski down to the road and take it back east towards Peaceful Valley and Hwy. 72. This makes a useful fast descent should it be necessary. Beware of snowmobilers on the road however, as it is one of their favorite trails. A second car (or lift) will be required to retrieve the vehicle from Beaver Reservoir if you follow the latter course. This route will make the trail around 8 miles in length.

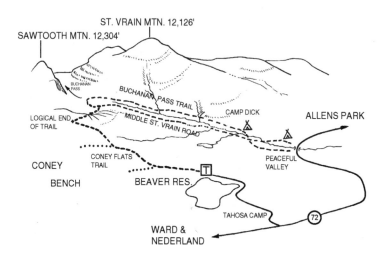

Left Hand Park Reservoir

Distance: 1½ miles one way
Difficulty: Easy
Time required: Half day
Blue Diamond Blazed: No
Start Elevation: 10,050' **Elevation Gain:** 570'

The trail with the longest name in this guide, it is a 'quickie' often used by late arrivals. The authors have even ascended in the last hour of daylight, and enjoyed a 'headtorch descent'.

Starts at Red Rock Trailhead, on the Brainard Lake Road. From Nederland, drive north on Hwy. 72 to just past Ward, where a road leads off to the left for Brainard Lake. Follow this for about 2½ miles to the trailhead. The road is closed to vehicles just ahead of this point during the winter months.

Trail follows the Reservoir Road to Left Hand Reservoir. It has a sheltered start in the trees, but is more exposed to the wind near the end. Snow drifts are often encountered near the reservoir. The middle section of the trail can appear to be a quite steep descent to the novice on the return trip, but is not really that bad! On a calm day, the northern slope of Bald Mountain, above the reservoir, can provide the skier with good practice at untracked skiing. Take advantage!

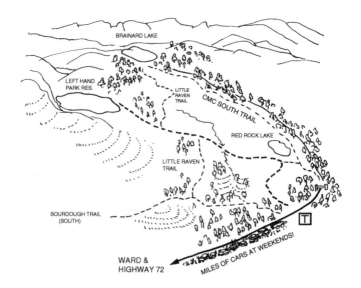

Little Raven Trail

Distance: 3 miles one way
Difficulty: Difficult
Time required: Half day
Blue Diamond Blazed: Yes, except for a short section
Start Elevation: 10,050' **Elevation Gain:** 510'

Dedicated to Chief Little Raven*. This trail contains only a short steep section, and this can be avoided on the return by taking the Left Hand Park Reservoir road back down to the trailhead.

Park at the Red Rock Trailhead, on the Brainard Lake Road. From Nederland, drive north on Hwy. 72 to just past Ward, where a road leads off to the left for Brainard Lake. Follow this for about 2½ miles to the trailhead. The road is closed to vehicles just ahead of this point during the winter months.

The trail actually starts ½ mile south of the trailhead off the Sourdough Trail. From the junction with the Sourdough Trail, strike out west up the steep trail to join the Left Hand Park Reservoir Road. Follow the road south for about a ½ mile, then leave it heading west on fairly level terrain to a final gentle descent to the Chief Little Raven Monument. From here you can either retrace your tracks, take the CMC South Trail home, or cross a meadow to the north in order to join with the Brainard Lake Road.

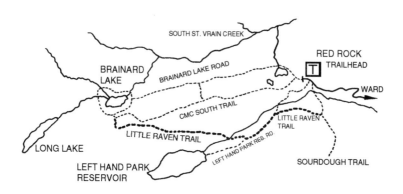

* *Little Raven was chief of the Southern Arapahoe Indians. On his death in 1889 he was succeeded by Chief Niwot, also known as Left Hand.*

CMC South Trail

Distance:	2 miles one way
Difficulty:	Easy
Time required:	Half day
Blue Diamond Blazed:	Yes

Start Elevation: 10,050' **Elevation Gain:** 370'

The most straightforward trail in this area. A jaunt through the woods to the monument dedicated to Chief Little Raven.

Park at the Red Rock Trailhead, on the Brainard Lake Road. From Nederland, drive north on Hwy. 72 to just past Ward, where a road leads off to the left for Brainard Lake. Follow this for about 2½ miles to the trailhead. The road is closed to vehicles just ahead of this point during the winter months.

Ski past the closure gate on the Brainard Lake Road and continue on for about 50 yards, then break left on a mainly level trail that ends at a junction with the Little Raven Trail. Either return the same way, or head north across a meadow for a few hundred yards (not blazed) to the Brainard Lake Road.

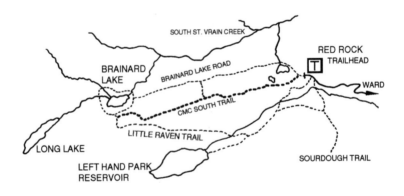

Safety Tip
For the novice or the unfit - it is always a good idea to choose a trip that is 'out and back' so that it can be cut short at any time.

Jean Lunning Scenic Trail

Distance: 3½ miles one way
Difficulty: Moderate
Time required: Full day
Blue Diamond Blazed: Partially
Start Elevation: 10,050' **Elevation Gain:** 610'

This trail, a popular summer walk, makes a fine winter trip as it loops around Long Lake.

Park at the Red Rock Trailhead, on the Brainard Lake Road. From Nederland, drive north on Hwy. 72 to just past Ward, where a road leads off to the left for Brainard Lake. Follow this for about 2½ miles to the trailhead. The road is closed to vehicles just ahead of this point during the winter months.

Ski the Brainard Lake Road to Brainard Lake, then follow the road around to the north to the Long Lake Trailhead. From here, enter the trees and follow the trail for several hundred yards to a clearing. Cross the creek on the left using a bridge, then continue on around to the south-west, keeping Long Lake on your right. The loop parallels the lake, most of the time in the trees, and continues on past the end of the lake for about another ½ mile before curling back around to the north to re-join the Long Lake Trail. At the junction, it is only a ½ mile west to Lake Isabelle where you'll be rewarded with tremendous views of Navajo, Apache and Shoshoni peaks. If time is short, at the junction with the Long Lake Trail, turn right instead, and follow this back eastwards to the Long Lake Trailhead.

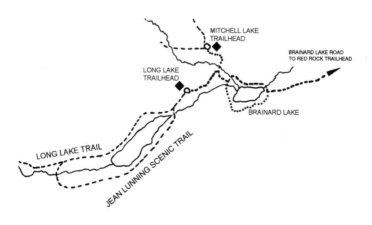

Sourdough Trail - Northern Section
Brainard Lake Road to Beaver Reservoir

Distance: 6 miles one way
Difficulty: Moderate
Time required: Full day
Blue Diamond Blazed: Yes
Start Elevation: 10,050' **Elevation Gain:** -900'

The complete Sourdough Trail is about 14 miles in length, from the Rainbow Lakes Road to the Middle St. Vrain Road near Peaceful Valley. It is better, however, to do it in two sections.

Park at the Red Rock Trailhead, on the Brainard Lake Road. From Nederland, drive north on Hwy. 72 to just past Ward, where a road leads off to the left for Brainard Lake. Follow this for about 2½ miles to the trailhead. The road is closed to vehicles just ahead of this point during the winter months.

This well-marked trail drops into St. Vrain Valley, crosses the South St. Vrain Creek, then turns west on the South St. Vrain Trail. Follow this to a junction where the Sourdough Trails heads north, then more easterly again until you reach the Beaver Reservoir Road. From there you can either continue straight on to Peaceful Valley on the final section of the Sourdough Trail; turn around and return; or head east on the Beaver Reservoir Road to meet the Peak to Peak Highway just over a mile further (In which case a car shuttle is required).

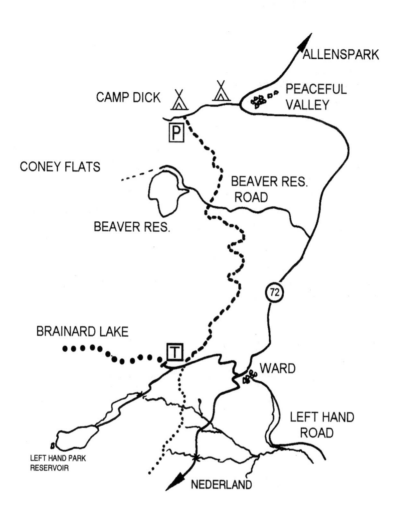

Sourdough Trail - Southern Section
Brainard Lake Road to Rainbow Lakes Road

Distance: 5½ miles one way
Difficulty: Moderate
Time required: Full day
Blue Diamond Blazed: Yes
Start Elevation: 10,050' **Elevation Gain:** 160'

An easy-angled trail with an enjoyable final descent to the Mountain Research Station, and limited, yet pleasant views. At the trail end, you are 1,350' lower than your start point. A car shuttle is preferable to skiing back up the hill.

Park at the Red Rock Trailhead, on the Brainard Lake Road. From Nederland, drive north on Hwy. 72 to just past Ward, where a road leads off to the left for Brainard Lake. Follow this for about 2½ miles to the trailhead. The road is closed to vehicles just ahead of this point during the winter months.

Head southward passing the Little Raven Trail junction on the right after less than ½ mile. Continue on, past a viewpoint of the plains out east; then after 2½ miles the trail takes a sharp left, and zig-zags in and out of the Upper Four Mile Creek. There is possible avalanche danger from the slopes above in this area. Gradually the trail descends and curves around in a south-easterly direction. Avoid taking the road that leads to the University of Colorado Mountain Research Station. Instead, swing round to the left and descend beyond, finishing up at the Rainbow Lakes Road.

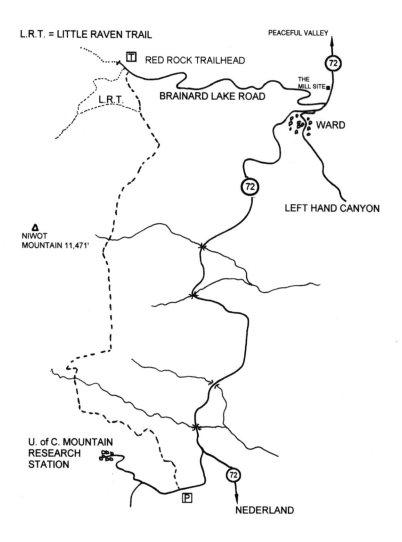

L.R.T. = LITTLE RAVEN TRAIL

PEACEFUL VALLEY

RED ROCK TRAILHEAD

72

L.R.T.

THE MILL SITE

BRAINARD LAKE ROAD

WARD

72

LEFT HAND CANYON

NIWOT MOUNTAIN 11,471'

72

U. of C. MOUNTAIN RESEARCH STATION

P

72

NEDERLAND

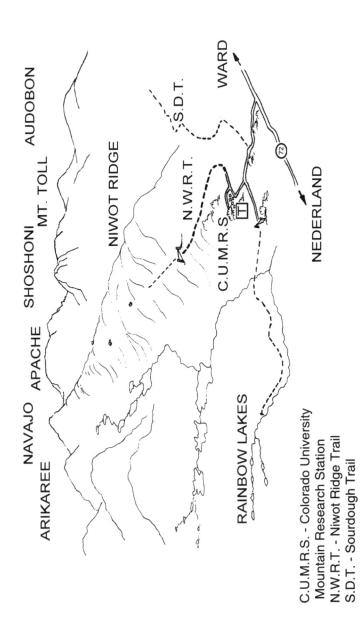

C.U.M.R.S. - Colorado University
Mountain Research Station
N.W.R.T. - Niwot Ridge Trail
S.D.T. - Sourdough Trail

Niwot Ridge

Distance:	3 miles one way
Difficulty:	Moderate
Time required:	Half day (Full day to the ridge)
Blue Diamond Blazed:	No

Start Elevation: 9,520'   **Elevation Gain:** 1,480'

Getting up on the ridge can take on expedition-like proportions when visibility is poor, or in high winds. But on those calm sunny days, the views are superb. You'll also see the out-of-bounds water catchment area for Boulder. It is interesting to note that Boulder is the only city in the USA that owns it's own glacier - the Arapahoe Glacier.

Starts from the east side of the University of Colorado Mountain Research Station, one mile west on the Rainbow Lakes Road from Hwy. 72, seven miles north of Nederland.

From the Research Station buildings, the trail goes initially northeast as it curves around following the jeep trail through the trees. It soon swings back around to head west, gradually climbing as it goes. Most will want to stop at the road closure gate after the 3½ mile point, and it is a nice spot for lunch. It is possible to ski beyond the gate, although the terrain and weather will influence your forward motion! Please observe the signs regarding closed areas as much research is done hereabouts. Walking is often the best alternative, and those that persist on up to the Niwot Ridge will be rewarded with good views of the Lake Isabelle area on the other side. The skiing on the ridge itself is generally not too good as it tends to get wind scoured.

Lunch on the Niwot Ridge Trail

Woodland Lake

Distance:	5 miles one way
Difficulty:	Difficult
Time required:	Full day
Blue Diamond Blazed:	No

Start Elevation: 8,750'   **Elevation Gain:** 2,280'

Not a route for your first outing of the season! Untracked conditions can give you even more of a workout. The views of the unnamed mountains in the upper basins above Woodland Lake are truly photogenic. Bring a camera!

From Nederland, drive south on Hwy. 72 for a short distance before taking a right towards Eldora. Drive through Eldora and park at the end of the ploughed road.

From the town, head out west following the road to a junction after about a mile. Take the left fork which leads to the Hessie town site. Keep heading west for a good ½ mile until a sign points south to Lost Lake. Continue on west. After a few hundred yards, a left fork heads towards King Lake. Go right, following Jasper Creek for about a mile to where a sign points left to Woodland Lake. The trail then rises for 2 miles up to the Lake. Avalanche danger often exists along this section of the trail so check conditions before setting out.

For a map see the King Lake Trail, page 44.

Always let your partner carry the gear!

Devils Thumb Lake

Distance: 7 miles one way
Difficulty: Difficult - an advanced trail
Time required: Full day
Blue Diamond Blazed: No
Start Elevation: 8,750'   **Elevation Gain:** 2,500'

This trail offers great views across the Continental Divide, but you'll have to work hard to get there! Most parties prefer to make the lake their final destination.

From Nederland, drive south on Hwy. 72 for a short distance before taking a right towards Eldora. Drive through Eldora and park at the end of the ploughed road.

Follow the trail west. After almost a mile, take the left fork towards the townsite of Hessie. Keep going west then follow the valley as it turns north-west up Jasper Creek. Where the slope angle steepens, the trail heads up the north slope and then west again, passing Jasper Lake on the right to a final steep section up to the Devils Thumb Lake.

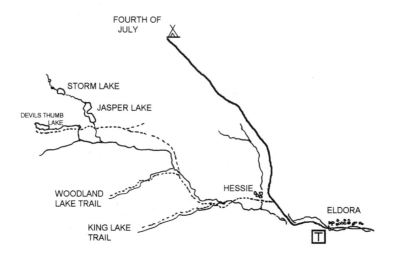

King Lake

Distance:	6 miles one way
Difficulty:	Difficult
Time required:	Full day
Blue Diamond Blazed:	No
Start Elevation: 8,750'	**Elevation Gain:** 2,150'

Begins on a snow-covered road and ends up on an undefined trail. The route takes you close to, and below, the Moffat Road Tunnel and Rollins Pass.

From Nederland, drive south on Hwy. 72 for a short distance before taking a right towards Eldora. Drive through Eldora and park at the end of the ploughed road.

Trail heads west from the parking area. After 1 mile, take the left fork towards the Hessie townsite. Keep heading west for another 1½ miles until a sign points south to Lost Lake. Continue west and soon after there is a registration box. The left branch follows the South Fork Creek for almost 4 miles up to the King Lake. There is avalanche danger along the final section of the trail so check conditions before setting out.

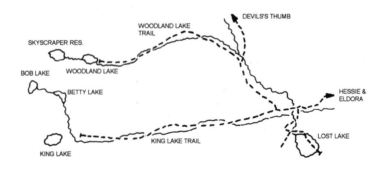

Lost Lake

Distance:	2½ miles one way
Difficulty:	Moderate
Time required:	Half day
Blue Diamond Blazed:	No
Start Elevation: 8,750'	**Elevation Gain:** 1,030'

A pleasant outing to a hidden lake. Short and sweet!

From Nederland, drive south on Hwy. 72 for a short distance before taking a right towards Eldora. Drive through Eldora and park at the end of the ploughed road.

Trail heads west from town along the unploughed road. After 1 mile, take the left fork towards the Hessie townsite. Keep heading west for another 1½ miles until a sign points south to Lost Lake. A steep ascent leads up to the lake.

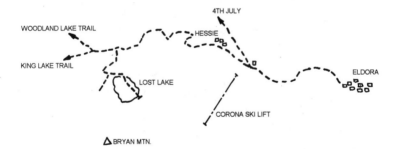

Fourth of July

Distance:	5 miles one way
Difficulty:	Easy
Time required:	Full day
Blue Diamond Blazed:	No
Start Elevation: 8,750'	**Elevation Gain:** 1,380'

An ideal introduction to the sport, this trail can be cut short at any time. There are good views of the South Arapahoe Peak which dominates the scenery. Two miles beyond the campground is the Fourth of July Mine where silver, and later copper, were mined. A popular story for the naming of the mine is that silver was first discovered here on this day in 1872.

From Nederland, drive south on Hwy. 72 for a short distance before taking a right towards Eldora. Drive through Eldora and park at the end of the ploughed road.

Ski west along the unploughed road to the Hessie junction. Go right and follow the gentle uphill jeep track to the Fourth of July Campground.

Falling about in the snow

Jenny Creek

Distance:	4½ miles one way
Difficulty:	Easy
Time required:	Full day
Blue Diamond Blazed:	Yes
Start Elevation: 9,200'	**Elevation Gain:** 1,500

A well-proven classic, the final destination is Yankee Doodle Lake, a pleasant place for a picnic.

Starts at the Eldora Ski Resort. From Nederland, head south for a short distance on Hwy. 72 before turning right for Eldora. After 1 mile take the left turn, and follow for another 2 miles up to the resort. The trail begins at the side of the Ho Hum Beginners Chairlift.

Ski up the left side of the slope to the top of the chairlift. From here, keep an eye out for the National Forest Access signs that take you through the upper ski area. Then make a descending traverse to Jenny Creek. Head west up the valley for several hundred yards until the Guinn Mountain Trail (see page 48) turns right. Avoid this turn and continue west, following the creek. The trail breaks away from the creek eventually. A short steep section leads to a more gentle ascent around the south side of Guinn Mountain. Ski on over several hillocks to finish at the wonderfully named Yankee Doodle Lake.

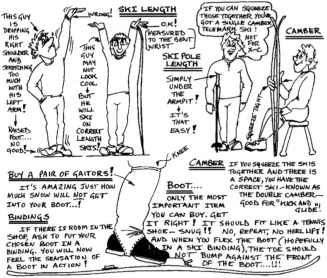

Quick tips on choosing skis

Guinn Mountain

Distance:	5 miles one way
Difficulty:	Difficult
Time required:	Full day
Blue Diamond Blazed:	Yes

Start Elevation: 9,200'   **Elevation Gain:** 2,000'

Starts at the Eldora Ski Resort. From Nederland, head south for a short distance before turning right for Eldora. After 1 mile take the left turn, and follow for another 2 miles up to the resort.

Ascend left by the side of the Ho Hum Beginners Chairlift to gain the ridge. Then go right, following an uphill trail away from the resort (going west), and ascend for about a mile. A descending traverse leads to a meadow to pick up a trail above and north of Jenny Creek. Follow the steep jeep road for ¼ mile taking a cut-off to the right on the Guinn Mountain Trail. From now on it's a steady uphill climb all the way to the logical destination - the Arestua* Hut. This was known in years gone by as the Guinn Mountain Hut and is maintained by the Colorado Mountaineering Club. Turn around and return.

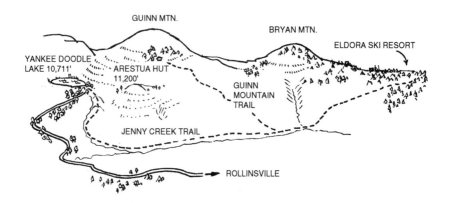

Arestua - Norwegian for shelter

Jenny Lind Gulch

Distance:	2 miles one way
Difficulty:	Easy
Time required:	Half day
Blue Diamond Blazed:	No

Start Elevation: 8,800'   **Elevation Gain:** 1,670'

Don't confuse Jean Lunning or Jenny Creek with Jenny Lind. Jenny Lind was one of Sweden's most famous operatic performers, unlike the other two!

Take Hwy. 119 to Nederland then follow Hwy. 72 south towards Central City. Where Hwy. 72 goes off left to Wondervu, continue on Hwy. 119 until Rollinsville (20 miles from Boulder). At Rollinsville take a right towards East Portal. Follow for 4 miles to a small parking recess by a gate. Look for a distinctive sign nailed to a tree (shown below). Do not block the gate.

From the trailhead, ski south, avoiding an early fork off to the left which goes to private property. Negotiate a creek at 1 mile, then steeply up the hillside for a further 1 mile or so. There is a large open bowl that gives excellent skiing after a new snowfall. Turn around and head back down. The hillside to the west offers an alternate descent. It is also possible to extend the day by exploring the mining roads to the east of the high point.

The Jenny Lind Gulch distinctive sign

Forest Lakes

Distance: 3½ miles one way
Difficulty: Difficult
Time required: Full day
Blue Diamond Blazed: No
Start Elevation: 9,590'   **Elevation Gain:** 1,230'

The Continental Divide is only a ½ mile away to the west from the end of this trail. The mountain circuit in this region is a total "Rocky Mountain Experience".

Take Hwy. 119 to Nederland then follow Hwy. 72 south towards Central City. Where Hwy. 72 goes off left to Wondervu, continue on Hwy. 119 until Rollinsville (20 miles from Boulder). At Rollinsville take a right towards East Portal. There is ample parking here, do not block the railway lines.

Walk across the railway and start your skiing. Take the access road to the left of the tunnel and keep the South Boulder Creek on your left. The junction with Arapahoe Creek is a ½ mile further on. A large open area is another ½ mile further where the trail forks. This is a good spot to picnic. Take the right fork and head steeply northeast, crossing Arapahoe Creek. The trail turns north-westerly, continuing uphill through the upper meadows to reach the lakes.

Winter mountain scene above the Forest Lakes

Meyers Homestead

Distance: 2½ miles one way
Difficulty: Easy
Time required: Half day
Blue Diamond Blazed: No
Start Elevation: 7,440'   **Elevation Gain:** 455'

The Meyers Homestead Trail is a pleasant ski through trees and meadows past the old homestead site. Great mountain views.

Trail is on the Walker Ranch. From Boulder, take Baseline up over Flagstaff and on past Kossler Lake. Walker Ranch is about 5 miles out of town. Starts at the trailhead and group picnic area on the right, just before the left turn to the Walker Ranch Historic Site.

Enjoy this gentle trip on a wide trail through the open valley ending at the scenic overlook.

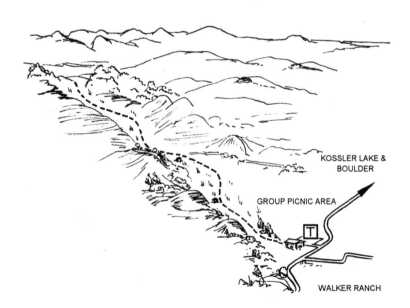

Eldora Nordic Center

PO Box 1378, Nederland. CO 80466 Telephone: (303) 440-8700

Trail Passes (1993-94 Season)

Adult	Full Day	$9
Seniors (65-69)	Full Day	$6
Seniors (70+)		FREE
Child (6 & Under)		FREE
Child (7-12)		$6

Ski rental and lessons are available.

25 miles of trails at Eldora are wide and groomed. A further 20 miles of ungroomed back country trails are also available.

Eldora Nordic Center
Photo:Eldora/Tim Hancock

Avalanches

Avalanches can occur without warning on almost any slope where snow has accumulated. This is especially true on the leeward or sheltered side of a slope. The presence of trees is no guarantee that the snow cannot slide. Once the snow does slide, be under no illusions - getting out can be almost impossible. The risk from avalanche can be greatly reduced by - listening to the avalanche reports, by being observant about your surroundings and by reading about them. In Boulder, Neptune Mountaineering and Mountain Sports both have free pamphlets on this complex subject.

USEFUL TELEPHONE NUMBERS

Weather and Snow conditions	(303) 236-9435
Denver area weather forecast	(303) 393-3964
State Patrol Road Conditions	(303) 639-1111
The Colorado Avalanche Information Center	(303) 275-5360

First Aid

To give advice on First Aid is not the object of this book, but it is our advice to pick up the telephone and enquire about taking a simple First Aid Course. Do not be afraid of your ignorance in this matter. Take the time to attend a clinic and you will feel much more confident in your outlook towards accidents in the outdoors. It sure beats standing around feeling helpless when an accident does occur. To avoid this feeling you may want to contact one of the following organizations.

HeartSmart offers customized first aid and CPR courses, with particular emphasis on backcountry travel.

They can be contacted at (303) 456-8543.

Bryan Mountain Nordic Ski Patrol offer three day courses in Avalanche and Mountaineering training.

For more information call (303) 443-6170.

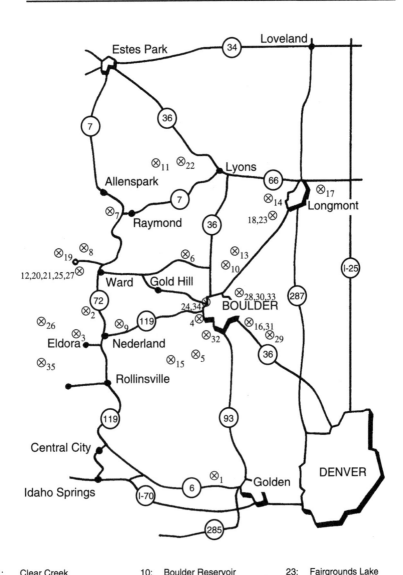

1:	Clear Creek	10:	Boulder Reservoir	23:	Fairgrounds Lake
2:	North Boulder Creek	11:	Buttonrock Reservoir	24:	Maxwell Lake
3:	Middle Boulder Creek,	12:	Brainard Lake	25:	Moraine Lake
	Upper section.	13:	Coot Lake	26:	Rainbow Lakes
4:	Middle Boulder Creek,	14:	Golden Park Ponds	27:	Red Rock Lake
	Lower section.	15:	Gross Reservoir	28:	Sawhill Ponds
5:	South Boulder Creek.	16:	Harper Lake	29:	Stearns Lake
6:	Lefthand Creek	17:	Jimm Hamm Nature Area	30:	Teller Lake
7:	St. Vrain Creek,	18:	Lagerman Reservoir	31:	Thunderbird
	Middle section.	19:	Lake Isabelle	32:	Viele Reservoir
8:	St. Vrain Creek,	20:	Lefthand Creek Reservoir	33:	Walden Ponds
	South section	21:	Long Lake	34:	Wonderland Lake
9:	Barker Reservoir	22:	Longmont Detention Res.	35:	Yankee Doodle Lake

Fishing

There are ample opportunities to fish in the Boulder area. Whilst none of the locations can truly be called 'Classic', they do offer considerable sport, and range from town reservoirs and ponds, to high mountain streams and lakes.

In this section, we have covered a vast area with the help of local enthusiasts in order to provide a selection of some of the best local fishing. The technicalities of the sport, for example - should one use a worm for Boulder Creek, or would a fly be better - are really the domain of an expert, definitely not us. The local fishing stores are a useful source of such additional information. See Reference 3.

Two types of waters are covered (a) warm waters - these are mainly reservoirs and ponds containing, typically bass and sunfish, and (b) cold waters, where trout would be prevalent. Boulder Reservoir has both warm and cold water fish because, due to its large size, it has different temperature zones.

A fishing license is required to fish in the state of Colorado, and this requirement is enforced. The fee is currently $20.25 for residents, more for non-residents. They are readily available at sport shops in the town. Of the license fee, 25 cents goes towards search and rescue operations. The Colorado Department of Wildlife will pay for your rescue costs should you need extracting from a tricky situation. Many a hiker and backcountry skier in the state has been sensible enough to purchase a fishing license for this reason.

Creeks

Clear Creek

Fish: Rainbow, brook and brown trout.
Information: The fish are wild and intelligent!
Special Restrictions: No

North Boulder Creek

Fish: Rainbow trout, brown trout and sucker.
Information: Sections of the creek run through private property. Probably the best fishing is to be found at the Rainbow Lakes. (Access is by a rough road - not for the sedate sedan!)
Special Restrictions: No

Middle Boulder Creek - Headwaters to Barker Reservoir

Fish: Rainbow trout, brown trout and sucker.
Information: Headwaters in the Roosevelt National Forest are open to public. Some areas are private and marked as such. At the Hessie trailhead, the stream is small and the fish wild!
Special Restrictions: No

Middle Boulder Creek - Barker Reservoir through Boulder City

Fish: Rainbow trout, brown trout and sucker.
Information: A unique opportunity for in-town fishing.
Special Restrictions: Yes - From end of Ebine Fine Park to 55th Street.
i)   Fishing by artificial flies & artificial lures only.
ii)   All fish must be released back to the water immediately.

South Boulder Creek

Fish: Rainbow trout, brown trout, brook trout and sucker.
Information: Walker Ranch section provides excellent fishing with diverse waters for the advanced fisherman. The creek seems to be dead about 1½ miles below Eldorado Canyon, but above it teems with wild fish.

Special Restrictions: Yes - From Walker Ranch to the South Boulder Road, and private land between Walker Ranch and Eldorado Canyon.
The section within Walker Ranch (2½ miles) is periodically stocked with rainbow trout. Fishing by both bait and flies permitted.

Lefthand Creek

Fish: Rainbow and brook trout.
Information: Small fish. Sometimes the water level falls so low that the fish die.
Special Restrictions: No

St Vrain Creek - Middle Section

Fish: Rainbow trout and cutbows.
Information: Supreme fishing, especially above Peaceful Valley. Has Cutbows galore! (Cutbows are a crossbreed of Cutthroats and Rainbow trout.)
Special Restrictions: No

St Vrain Creek - South Section

Fish: Rainbow trout.
Information: Stocked with fish. Good "Pocket Water" fishing.
Special Restrictions: Yes
Upstream from the bridge at the inlet of Brainard Lake to headwaters.
i)   Fishing by artificial flies & artificial lures only.
ii)   Bag limit for trout is 2 fish, 12" or longer with possession limit 7 fish.

Lakes and Reservoirs

Barker Reservoir

380 acres
Fish: Rainbow Trout, brown trout and sucker.
Information: There is good bait fishing at the inlet.
Special Restrictions: Yes - No ice fishing. No boats.
Directions: Just before Nederland on Boulder Canyon Rd - Hwy 119, 15 miles west out of Boulder.

Boulder Reservoir

540 acres
Fish: Walleye, yellow perch, crappie, largemouth bass, channel catfish.
Information: Gate Fees - Effective May 29th 1993:

Senior (65+)	Free
Senior (60-64 yrs)	$1.50
Adult (19+)	$3.50
Teen (13-18)	$2.25
Child (6-12)	$1.50
Child (under 6)	Free

Season Permits available.
Open Daily - Dawn to Dusk.
Tel Main Office: 441-3461
There is good bait fishing at the north inlet and at the east dam.
Special Restrictions: No
Directions: 2 miles north on Diagonal towards Longmont. Take a left at Jay, then take 51st almost immediately. Drive north on 51st for 1½ miles. Reservoir is off to the right.

Buttonrock Reservoir

375 acres
Fish: Trout.
Information: A permit from the City of Longmont is required. Lower down in Longmont Reservoir and the stream below it, no pass is required.
Special Restrictions: Yes
i)   Fishing by artificial flies & artificial lures only
ii)   Bag & possession limit for trout is 2 fish.
iii)   Fishing prohibited 11/1 - 4/30

Directions: Take Hwy. 36 to Lyons. At the junction with Hwy 66, head towards Estes Park. Drive through Lyons and about 2½ miles beyond, take CR. 80. Buttonrock Reservoir is some 4 miles further on.

Wet Fly (Left)
Tends to be more compact than the dry fly, and is flat in appearance. Designed to sink immediately in the water.

Dry Fly (Right)
Has hackle fibers projecting at right angles, enabling the fly to float on the surface.

FLIES

Brainard Lake

15.6 acres
Fish: Rainbow trout, brown trout, brook trout.
Information: Pretty good fishing, but the nearby lakes - especially Red Rock Lake - are better.
Special Restrictions: No
Directions: From Nederland, take Hwy. 72 north to Ward. Just past Ward take the left turn sign posted for Brainard Lake. Follow this road for 4 miles to Brainard Lake.

Coot Lake

10 acres
Fish: Bass and bluegills.

Information: Once popular with nude sunbathers, fishermen can keep their clothes on, at least whilst casting.

Special Restrictions: No

Directions: N. 63rd, 2 miles north of Hwy. 119. Just the other side of the Boulder Reservoir. Take Diagonal to wards Niwot. Just before Niwot, take a left onto N.63rd. Coot Lake is ¾ mile further, on the left.

Golden Park Ponds

94 acres

Fish: Trout, perch and largemouth bass.

Information: Good for lures and flies.

Special Restrictions: Yes

Pond #1 i)   Fishing by artificial flies & artificial lures only

         ii)   Largemouth & smallmouth bass must be released if under 15 inches.

Ponds #2,3,4   i)   Largemouth & smallmouth bass must be released if under 15 inches.

Directions: East of Hover Road in Longmont. Located at 2651 Third Avenue.

Gross Reservoir

412 acres

Fish: Rainbow trout, lake trout, kokanee salmon, tiger muskie.

Information: Steep banks.

Special Restrictions: Yes

i)   No fishing between 9pm - 4am or as posted.

Directions: 9 miles south-west of Boulder off Flagstaff Drive.

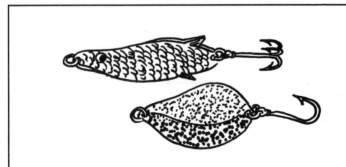

Spoons - designed to produce a wriggling motion

Harper Lake

16 acres

Fish: Rainbow trout.

Information: Lake is stocked with rainbow trout in the spring, by fall they are all gone!

Special Restrictions: No

Directions: N. McCaslin Blvd in west Louisville.

Spinner - has a loose blade or plate which makes it spin. Different shaped plates make it spin faster or slower.

Jim Hamm Nature Area

12 acres

Fish: Trout.

Information: Probably the most heavily stocked area in Colorado.

Special Restrictions: No

Directions: East of Longmont at 17th Ave. & County Line Road.

Lagerman Reservoir

116 acres

Fish: Largemouth bass, walleye, black crappie, bluegill and channel catfish.

Information: Bank & boat fishing allowed.

Special Restrictions: Yes

i)   Largemouth & smallmouth bass must be released if under 15 inches.

Directions: 4 miles south-west of Longmont on Pike Rd.

Lake Isabelle

30 acres

Fish: Rainbow trout.

Information: Non-motorized boats only. Float tubes ok.

Special Restrictions: Yes
i)   Fishing by artificial flies & artificial lures only.
ii)   Bag, possession & size limit for trout is 2 fish, 12" or longer.
Directions: Lake Isabelle lies in the Indian Peaks Wilderness. From Nederland, take Hwy. 72 north to Ward. Just past Ward take the left turn sign posted for Brainard Lake. Follow this road past Brainard Lake, and take the second right for the Long Lake Trailhead. Park here. The lake is approached by taking the trail past Long Lake and continuing west for another 1½ miles.

Lefthand Creek Reservoir

100 acres
Fish: Rainbow trout, brook trout and brown trout.
Information: Boats allowed.
Special Restrictions: No
Directions: From Nederland, take Hwy. 72 north to Ward. Just past Ward take the left turn sign posted for Brainard Lake. Drive along here for 2 miles to the Red Rock Trailhead.The road to the Reservoir goes off to the left from here. Unsurfaced road, suitable for high clearance vehicles.

Long Lake

39.5 acres
Fish: Rainbow trout.
Information: The outlet creek is also fishable. The lake is marshy so bring deet to ward off ferocious insects.
Special Restrictions: Yes
i)   Largemouth and smallmouth bass must be released if under 15".
ii)   Bag, possession & size limit for trout is 2 fish, 12" or longer.
iii)   Fishing prohibited upstream from bridge at inlet of Brainard Lake to Long Lake (5/1 - 7/15).
Directions: From Nederland, take Hwy. 72 north to Ward. Just past Ward take the left turn, sign posted for Brainard Lake. Follow this road past Brainard Lake, and take the second right for the Long Lake

---

TIP: Flies that work in the Boulder area.

Wet Fly - try Tan Hare's Ear Nymph
Dry Fly - try Elk Hair Caddis Dry Fly
These really will work!

Trailhead. Park here. The lake is approached by taking the trail leading from the trailhead. The lake is about a ½ mile walk.

Longmont Detention Reservoir

3 acres
Fish: Trout.
Special Restrictions: No
Directions: Take Hwy. 36 to Lyons. At the junction with Hwy 66, head towards Estes Park. Drive through Lyons and about 2½ miles beyond, take CR. 80. The Reservoir is about 2 miles further, and about halfway to Buttonrock Reservoir.

Longmont Fairgrounds Lake

16 acres
Fish: Largemouth bass, bluegill and channel catfish.
Information: Very good for bass and the night fishing is said to be excellent. There is also Cattail Pond which is for children only.
Special Restrictions: Yes
i)   Fishing by artificial flies & artificial lures only.
ii)   All warm water fish must be released immediately.
Directions: Hover & Rogers Roads in Longmont.

Maxwell Lake

1.5 acres
Fish: Bluegill, bull head, largemouth bass, catfish and sucker.
Information: Small lake surrounded by trees making it almost impossible to fly cast.
Special Restrictions: No
Directions: North of Linden Avenue.

Moraine Lake

6.5 acres
Fish: Rainbow trout.
Information: Shallow water. The larger fish are renowned for being tricky to catch.
Special Restrictions: No
Directions: From Nederland, take Hwy. 72 north to Ward. Just past Ward take the left turn sign posted for Brainard Lake. Follow this road for 2 miles to Red Rock Trailhead. Moraine Lake lies just to the south of Red Rock Lake.

Rainbow Lakes

Ten lakes, 1 to 4 acres.

Fish: Rainbow and brook trout.

Information: Access road is rough, may not be suitable for all vehicles. Due to sediments, the lakes are unwadeable but there is good fishing from the banks.

Special Restrictions: No

Directions: The lakes are located west and south-west of the Rainbow Lakes campground. From Nederland, drive north on Hwy. 72 for 7 miles to a left turn, sign posted for the University of Colorado Mountain Research Station. Take this rough road and follow for 4 miles - ignore the right turn after about a mile which leads to the Research Station.

Red Rock Lake

6.5 acres

Fish: Rainbow trout.

Information: A favorite with many fishermen. The fish are a good size and easy to catch. A good place for beginners.

Special Restrictions: No

Directions: From Nederland, take Hwy. 72 north to Ward. Just past Ward take the left turn sign posted for Brainard Lake. Follow this road for 2 miles to the Red Rock Trailhead. Red Rock Lake lies just to the west of the trailhead.

Sawhill Ponds

16 ponds - total of 72 acres

Fish: Bluegill, bullhead, catfish, crappie, largemouth bass,sucker and yellow perch.

Information: The best ponds are Island Pond and Bass Pond. Huge carp can be caught here.

Special Restrictions: Yes

i)   Fishing by artificial flies & artificial lures only, except on ponds 1 & 1A.

ii)   Largemouth & smallmouth bass must be released if under 15".

Directions: 75th north of Valmont.

Stearns Lake

23 acres

Fish: Tiger muskie and channel catfish, also huge blue gills.

Information: No boating or wading as Stearns Lake is a critical wildlife habitat. The tiger muskie will require considerable patience!

Special Restrictions: No

Directions: On Rock Creek Farm at 104th and Dillon Roads south of Lafayette.

Teller Lake

22 acres

Fish: Bluegill, bullhead, carp, crappie, largemouth bass and yellow perch.

Information: Wonderful fishing fro spawning bluegills in May.

Special Restrictions: Yes

i)   Largemouth & smallmouth bass must be released if under 15".

Directions: ½ mile east of 75th St, and north of Arapahoe. Park at the Teller Farm Trailhead.

Thunderbird

2 acres

Fish: Bluegill , crappie, green sunfish and largemouth bass.

Information: Close to the center of town. Good family fishing.

Special Restrictions: No

Directions: South-east Boulder off Mohawk Drive.

Fly Fishing - the First Cast

Front Range fly fishing
Photo: Anne Krause

Viele Lake

6 acres
Fish: Bluegill, bullhead and carp.
Information: Reasonable fishing.
Special Restrictions: No
Directions: South Boulder off Gillaspie Drive.

Walden Ponds

5 ponds - 42 acres

Fish: Largemouth bass, channel catfish and bluegill.

Information: Fishing is better than at the adjoining Sawhill Ponds. Originally a gravel pit, Walden is now a wetland habitat with five ponds, all except Picnic Pond are catch and release. Artificial flies and lures only. No wading or boats.

Picnic Pond is restricted to Seniors and/or handicapped residents of Boulder County. Annual Permit required ($5). A feature of the Picnic Pond is a pier from which to fish. Picnic Pond is stocked with rainbow trout during the spring and fall.

Special Restrictions: Yes

i)   Fishing by artificial flies & artificial lures only.

ii)   Largemouth & smallmouth bass must be released immediately, except at Picnic Pond.

Directions: 6 miles north-east of Boulder on 75th.

Wonderland Lake

34 acres

Fish: Largemouth bass, crappie, bluegill and perch.

Information: Fishing is legal only on the east side of the lake. The west side is a wildlife sanctuary.

Special Restrictions: No

Directions: North Boulder off Wonderland Hill Road.

Yankee Doodle Lake

5 acres

Fish: Rainbow and brook trout.

Information: Rollins Pass Road may be blocked by snow into July. The South Boulder Creek is on the way up to the lake - fish on your way up there!

Special Restrictions: No

Directions: From Nederland, head south on Hwy. 72 to Rollinsville. Take the right on Forest Route 149 which leads to East Portal. Just before East Portal, take the rough road on the right which leads up the hillside. This is the Rollins Pass Road. The lake is some 10 miles further on.

Mountain bikes take to the air
Photo: Dan Guggenheim

Flying

If there was one wish many skiers would have as they battle their way across the Continental Divide on a snowy Friday night, heading for the ski resorts, it must be - "I wish there was a better way!"

Fortunately there is a better way. While not exactly cheap, it is possible to hire a pilot and light aircraft to take you into the mountains at a greater speed, with less stress and far better views. Light aircraft usually have room for up to five people and limited baggage, or less people and some real toys, like a mountain bike or two.

For instance, if you wanted to have a days skiing in Aspen, we have been quoted $250-$300 for the aircraft and pilot. Split between five people this makes a reasonably priced day out and is after all, not an inappropriate way to visit the town.

Other trips available locally include one hour trips over the Rockies. One operator will even take you and your family and turn the flight into a learning experience. Kids can learn about geography, hydrology, wildlife and ecosystems all from the air. A trip like that may run around $100 total. For the adventurous fisherman, the plane can be hired to check out those hidden fishing spots from the air, then trace back to the nearest trail. Visitors from out of town might like a short flight to see the aspen trees in all their glory in the Fall.

For the real enthusiast, a Pilot's License is probably the most liberating of all pieces of paper. It will require 50 hours flying time and cost anywhere between $3,200 and $4,000. Many Instructors will expect to see you two days a week and the longer you take, the more expensive it will become.

See Reference 3 for some phone numbers of local operators.

Tranquility over the Flatirons

Photo: Bruce Miller

Gliding

Boulder, due to it's proximity to the Front Range and the Rockies, offers one of the best sites in the country for gliding. Three aspects influence a good flight: ridge soaring, thermal activity and wave.

Ridge soaring can be done just west of Boulder at the start of the Foothills. Wind, coming from the east, hits the Foothills and is forced to rise to get over them. This rising air can then be used by pilots to gain height. Generally speaking, ridge lift does not provide the same amount of lift as thermal or wave lift, although it may be used in conjunction with them.

Thermal activity is caused by air at ground level warming to a temperature higher than the surrounding air, then rising. This mass of rising air can provide lift for light aircraft such as a sailplane, and enable the pilot to reach great heights. Thermalling is usually best in the Boulder area April through October.

Wave is the movement of air in a wave-like motion at high levels caused by mountains upwind from the site. The waves waft ever higher (again rising air), and allow the pilot not only to gain height but also to potentially travel great distances as well. It was from wave lift that local pilot, Jim Munn, set the Colorado State Altitude Record in 1977 by reaching 44,000 feet above sea level!

For the insatiably curious, one company in town offers glider flights. One of the nice things about these flights is that there are a number to choose from, depending on your need for excitement. A 'simple' scenic flight is a great way to get above the town and see over to the Continental Divide.

An Account of an Acrobatic Flight
by Mark Springett

The acrobatic flight provides a unique experience that is not for the faint hearted. Before you get into the 850lb aircraft, you are taught how to use the parachute, should it become necessary. You sit in front of the pilot, your head in a plexiglass dome well above the fuselage profile. There are controls in front of you. Take off is mundane - you are towed up to 10,000' or 11,000' feet above sea level, a mile or more above Boulder. Two waggles of the towplane wings and you release the tow and....goodbye motor.

On my first flight, the Swiss glider pilot seated behind me pointed the aircraft vertically down toward the farmland north of Boulder and we accelerated rapidly to about 150mph. He then pulled the aircraft vertically upwards in a face-crunching 5G turn, and let it go into a freefall hammerhead stall* - where the glider stops climbing and falls backward until the pilot can regain control. This maneuver was followed by a succession of loops, inverted flight and rolls that defied the description at the head of the section. The sound of wind over the aerofoils and the gravitational extremes provided by this exciting flight do not fit into the class of a 'peaceful nature'. If you are an adrenaline junkie, you will probably come back for another shot though!

The other rides offered are less nerve wracking, but each level of entertainment is well worth the effort and the rush.

* The authors understand that the hammerhead stall is no longer part of the acrobatic flight - shame!

Sports Injuries

Injuries are a common but unfortunate part of outdoor activities. Here are a few "rules of thumb" for preventing and treating common problems.

Prevention

Remember, most sports injuries can be prevented through proper conditioning and preparation. A regular exercise program will build strength, endurance and flexibility. For all athletic activities warm-up first, then gently stretch your muscles, ie. walk briskly for 5 minutes, stretch and then begin your activity.

Use appropriate athletic equipment properly adjusted for your body. If you already own the right gear, make sure it is regularly serviced. Those expensive ski bindings won't help prevent injuries if they are not properly adjusted, and even top-of-the-line mountain bikes need regular maintenance.

Many injuries can be prevented by staying alert and keeping a high energy level. Fatigue and dehydration can be avoided by taking frequent rest breaks, eating snacks regularly, and drinking fluids.

Treatment

RICE - Rest, Ice, Compression and Elevation - remember this acronym! It can help you treat those occasional mishaps and allow you to get back into action sooner.

REST - Rest the injured area as soon as possible.

ICE - Ice the injured area immediately. Cold should be left on for 15-20 minutes and used periodically during the first three days. It's a good idea to carry a chemical cold pack, if you don't have one, snow or a cold stream will do.

COMPRESSION - Carry a small ace bandage to wrap an injured area. This not only reduces swelling, but provides support. Always wrap towards the heart. For example, if you sprain your knee, wrap from below the joint in an upward direction to above the joint. Check periodically to make sure the bandage is not too tight.

ELEVATION - Elevate the injured area above the heart.

Anti-inflammatories such as asprin and ibuprofen also help reduce pain and swelling. These products are available in name brands such as Advil or Nuprin, or as generic equivalents.

After a serious injury or if an apparent minor injury persists or worsens, seek professional medical care. Don't be macho! The sooner you take care of an injury, the less likely it will develop into worse and the sooner you will be back on the trail.

The Center for Integrated Therapies, to whom we are grateful for this article, is located in downtown Boulder at 934 Pearl St, Suite D. They are a Holistic Physical Therapy Center offering a variety of treatments including physical therapy, rolfing, massage and yoga. They will be happy to provide more information and a free consultation. Telephone (303) 447-9939.

Trying our luck in Clear Creek Canyon

Gold Panning

The first prospectors arrived in the area in the late 1850's. On October 17th, 1858, a camp was established at the mouth of Boulder Canyon at a place now called Red Rocks. The first significant find of gold was on the 16th of January 1859, when it was discovered in a tributary of the Boulder Creek - Gold Run - near Gold Hill. The settlement of Gold Hill grew up on the site. Since that find, gold became a significant part of Boulder's history. As mining intensified, Boulder grew in importance as a supply town for the gold mining towns to the west.

Despite the history of exploitation, there is still plenty of gold to be found in the area. Granted, the average gold panning enthusiast will not make a fortune, but there is still fun to be had panning for small pieces of gold. It is by no means easy, but armed with a gold pan and a few pointers, most people should strike it lucky! It also has the advantage of being a very cheap activity with a possible payoff. Sure beats plying the slots in the gambling towns, and you get fresh mountain air to boot!

The first gold miners who came to the area would have used the trusty gold pan to check for the presence of gold. The simplicity and speed with which an area can be assessed are its main advantages. As the more obvious nuggets were extracted, more gravel had to be processed to get the same amount. For that reason, developments such as the rocker or cradle, and dredges which created the curved, ridged piles of tailings that can be seen in Clear Creek even to this day, came about. The rockers were simple boxes with meshes in them which would sort the dirt, allowing the heavy gold to fall through and be collected. Some modern day enthusiasts still use rockers and suction dredges, but most are content to use the tried and tested pan, although some prefer clear pyrex dishes - you can see the gold from underneath - and others opt for modern plastic pans with special lips to catch the gold. All types of gold pan from the simplest to the most sophisticated will probably work, provided you know the secrets of panning.

How to Pan for Gold

Gold pans can be bought locally at McGuckins on Folsom Street and start around $7. The plastic ones will not rust like the steel versions but do not look as good! It is also possible to buy a Gold Panning Kit which includes some useful tools such as a squeezer which is used to collect the tiny gold chips, and clear vial to hold them in. The kits also include a bag of gravel which is guaranteed to contain real gold, (there are no guarantees in gold panning so the gold contained therein is clearly not native!). The advantage of panning a pan or two of gravel known to contain gold is that you get a chance to hone your skills. For this reason, we recommend swallowing your pride and giving it a shot.

The first thing to understand about gold panning is that gold is dense. OK, that sounds rather obvious, but a common mistake of the first timer is to walk to the edge of a creek, grab a handful of nice, clean looking gravel from the creek bed and start swilling it around the pan. The problem is that most, if not all, the gold that you seek will have worked its way down through the lighter stuff and be down almost to the bedrock. So, you need to dig. Also, due to the force of the water, the gold tends to accumulate in the slower-moving parts of the creek such as the insides of bends and underneath large boulders. Another source of likely material will be from areas of bedrock exposed near the creek. Wherever it comes from, get a good amount into the pan and you are ready to sort out the muck from the gold.

The 'golden rule' is not to swirl the pan. Start by removing obvious large rocks and debris from the pan by hand. Then with plenty of water in the pan, start gently shaking the pan from side to side, allowing sand and gravel to gradually spill over the far side of the pan. By this method, the heavy gold will sink into the bottom of the pan, whilst the lighter stuff returns to the creek. As you work the pan, keep an eye on the material - particularly for gold looking specks (nuggets would be nice, but specks are more likely). Two things to watch out for are the infamous "fools gold" and mica. Fools Gold or pyrite, has a gold look about it, but, unlike gold, will not maintain its sheen when in the shade. Mica is common and has a glistening look to it. It can also float, which is a bit of a hint that it is not what you seek. As you get down to the last tablespoon of gravel you should have some black dust which is magnetite, and a good sign that you may be in the right area, and if luck is on your side, some gold chips about the size of this period. A magnet is useful for getting rid of the black sand - wrap it in thin plastic so it doesn't stick directly to the magnet. The best way to retrieve the gold is to use a sucker bottle or tweezers to remove it from the pan. A clear plastic vial is useful to keep the flecks in, and to display your finds in the bar later on. (Tip: Fill the vial with water - it acts like a magnifying glass and enhances the appearance of your discovery).

Armed with your pan and some basic information, the only thing left is to find a suitable spot. We are reliably informed that even Boulder Creek in town can be fruitful, but we doubt that a beginner will find much. More likely spots are the well known pull-ins along Clear Creek Canyon from Golden. There are almost always people trying their luck along the creek. Otherwise, check Reference 4 for recommend reading, or alternatively, start looking for your own spot! Finally, take care not to trespass - if the land is posted it is a good hint that your presence will be unwelcome. Public land is a better bet.

Oh, and good luck!

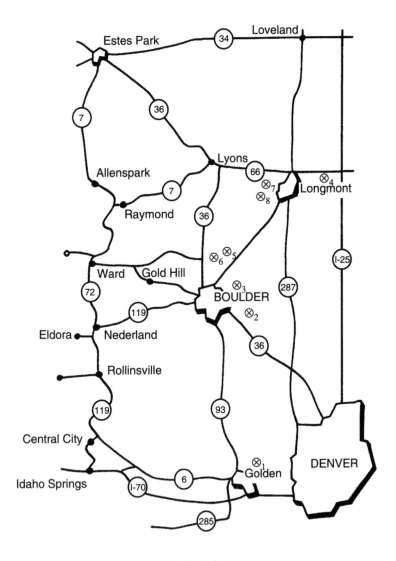

1:   Applewood Golf Course
2:   Coal Creek Golf Course
3:   Flatirons Golf Course
4:   Fox Hill Country Club
5:   Haystack Mountain Golf Course
6:   Lake Valley Golf Course
7:   Sunset Municipal Golf Course
8:   Twin Peaks Golf Course

Golf

History put golfs origins in Scotland, and sometimes more specifically, Muirfield, which preceded the more famous St. Andrews by about 50 years. There has been a tremendous local growth in golfing in recent years and the area now supports some 60 courses within a one hour drive. Two popular courses - Indian Peaks and Coal Creek are the latest additions.

Legend has it that golf balls fly further a mile high than they would at sea level. We suspect that this is more wishful thinking than anything else. What can be said however, is that, as with many Colorado golf courses, the mountains make a superb backdrop, and an early morning round just as the sun hits the Flatirons is said to be one of life's great pleasures!

Good weather helps in maintaining the popularity of the sport locally, and the enthusiast should be able to play pretty much year round.

We have picked a small selection of the golf courses in the area to list here. There are many more but we did not have the space to list them all. For information on the other courses, contact one of the golfing stores listed in Reference 2.

Applewood Golf Course. Golden.

14001 W. 32nd Ave, Golden. Tel: (303) 279-3003

A flat, wide open course, with some trees, lakes and bunkers. Quite a challenging course. Uniquely designed, Applewood is the only golf course in Colorado that is a member of the Audobon Society. For this, they meet the society's requirements of using no pesticides and have a reduced irrigation system.

18 hole course.
Fees:

18 holes	$17 (M - T)	$19 (F - S)
Cart: $9.50 per rider.		
Twilight Special:	After 4.00pm	$11.00
	After 6.30pm	$9.95*
	* Includes cart.	
Early Bird Special	Before 7.00am	$9.95*
	* Includes cart. (9 holes)	

Coal Creek Golf Course. Louisville.

585 W. Dillon Rd. Louisville. Tel: (303) 666-7888

The second highest golf course rating in Colorado. A scenic course with great views of the Flatirons. Coal Creek is a factor in 12 of its 18 holes.

18 hole championship course, 6,957 yds, driving range.

Fees	18 holes	9 holes
Non-Louisville Residents	$16.50	$10
Louisville Residents	$12 (M-T)	$8 (M - T)
	$14 (F - S)	$9 (F - S)

Flatirons Golf Course. Boulder.

5706 Arapahoe. Reservations & Pro Shop Tel: 442-7851

A municipal golf course with attached private club. A mature course with many lakes,trees and creeks. The abundant water,strategically placed bunkers and trees combine to provide a challenging and enjoyable golf experience.

Offering a lighted driving range, target greens, and a color-coded distance system. Instant Replay Video system available at no extra charge (Bring your own tape).

Player fees:

	City Resident*	Non-Resident
9 Holes	$9	$11
18 Holes	$13	$16
9 Holes (Junior/Senior)**	$6	$11
18 Holes (Junior/Senior)**	$8	$16
Annual Passes City Resident		Non-Resident
Adult	$295	$340
Jr/Sr	$145	N/A

Pass Holders pay reduced rate of $1.50/9 holes, $3.00/18 holes.

* $5.00 once only annual fee for Resident Discount Card required.

** Juniors - up to 18yrs. Seniors - 60yrs +

Fox Hill Country Club. Longmont.

12389, Highway 119, Longmont. Tel: (303) 772-1061

Built in 1972 and designed by Frank Hummel, the course is heavily wooded and challenging. The Club currently has 400 members.

Foxhill is a private club, guests and visitors must be accompanied by a member.

18 holes, 6,404 yds to Par 70 from the white tees - Regular Course.

6,860 yds from the blue tees - Championship Course.

Fees:	Weekdays	Weekends
18 holes	$25	$35

Haystack Mountain Golf Course. Longmont.

5877 Niwot Rd.   Tel: (303) 530-1400

Strictly a walk-on course, it is relaxing with no bunkers. Noted for the wildlife that can be seen whilst playing.

9 holes, 2,000 yds.

Fees:		
9 holes	$8 (weekdays)	$9 (weekends)
18 holes	$12	$13
Seniors (55+)		
9 holes	$5 (weekdays)	$7 (weekends)
18 holes	$9	$11

Golfer with Flatirons backdrop
Photo: Anne Krause

Lake Valley Golf Club. Boulder.

4400 Lake Valley Drive, Longmont. Tel: (303) 444-2114

This 6,750yd, Press Maxwell-designed championship layout course is in the Scottish Links-style and includes a driving range. PGA Professional available for individuals or groups.

Fees:

9 holes $12.00 (weekdays)	$16.00 (weekends)
18 holes $17.00	$21.00

Twilight Rate (2 hrs prior to dusk) $8
Lessons and carts available.

Sunset Municipal Golf Course. Longmont.

1900 Longs Peak Ave, Longmont. Tel: (303) 776-3122

A mature course, built in the 1920's. Has lots of trees and no level greens. A challenging course with narrow fairways.

9 holes course.

Fees: (9 holes)
Adults $8 (weekdays) $12 (weekends)
Seniors & Juniors $5 $9
Non-Residents $2 extra.

Lessons and carts available.

Twin Peaks Municipal Golf Course. Longmont.

1200 Cornell, Longmont. Tel: (303) 772-1722

Built 15 years ago, it is generally flat with great views towards the mountains. A difficult course with undulating terrain.

18 hole course, 6767 yds, driving range.

Fees:
9 holes (Longmont Residents) $8
18 holes $12
9 holes (Non- Residents) $9
18 holes $14
Juniors and Seniors
$6 (9 holes) $10 (18 holes)   Weekdays only.

Lessons and carts available.

"Room with a View"
Looking west from above the Boulder Foothills
Photo: Ed Goss

Hang Gliding

The sport of hang gliding developed from work carried out by Dr. Rogallo during the forties and fifties on kites. He filed a patent on a flexible kite in 1948, and from that grew a huge volume of research by his employers - NASA - on flexible wings. Two offshoots of this work were the steerable recovery canopies used by the Gemini space program, and more importantly for this sport, the Rogallo wing. Used and developed by many pioneers, early versions were towed behind cars or boats. Of fairly crude construction - bamboo, plastic and sticky tape - the pilot hung from the frame by his armpits (hence 'hang gliders') and hoped for the best. Development was often done over sand dunes to break the fall should the sticky tape be stressed beyond normal operating limits! During this time, the rule was 'Never fly higher than you care to fall'!

Since then the Rogallo wing has been extensively developed and the modern hang glider is a very safe and dependable aircraft. The sport has become very popular in the USA, perhaps more so here than anywhere else in the world. Two locally active pioneers in the sport - Scott Westfall from Boulder and Larry Tudor from Denver, have played key roles in the sport since its early days in the seventies.

The hang glider is a unique aircraft in that it is steered by weight shift. That is, the pilot uses his or her own body weight to turn the aircraft, unlike all other steerable aircraft where directional control is managed by the movement of wing surfaces to disrupt airflow and create drag.

In general, the best time of year for hang gliding along the

Front Range is March through to June, and often September and October as well.

Local pilots have often flown up to the legal altitude limit of 18,000' and accomplished many long distance flights. Notable amongst these is Ed Goss's flight from Boulder to Colorado Springs, a distance of 100 miles. Fort Collins and Larkspur have also been reached by local pilots - a distance of around 60 miles. These are not by any means world records, but impressive flights nonetheless.

Hang gliding should be seen as a sport which, for safety reasons, should only be entered into through proper instruction by a recognized training school.

Visiting pilots are recommended to join the Rocky Mountain Hang Gliding Association. They meet the third wednesday of every month at 7pm at Senór Frogs on Colfax in Golden. Due to changing site regulations, the association keeps abreast of these changes and other matters affecting local pilots. Contact them at (303) 980-0020.

A local contact in Boulder is Scott Westfall. He is a gear distributor and a useful source of information about flying locally. Scott can be contacted at (303) 444-5455.

The USHGA (United States Hang Gliding Association) oversees the sport nationally and is based in Colorado Springs. They can be contacted at (719) 632-8300.

For local weather and wind conditions, call (303) 799-7000 - access through #*212.

Local sites include:

Wonderland Hills in North Boulder.

It is recommended that you contact local pilots before flying from this site. It is possible to walk up the hill and take off. The top of the ridge is on private land and written permission must be sought before use.

Flagstaff Mountain, Boulder.

Rarely used, Flagstaff Mountain is a dramatic site overlooking Chautauqua Park and the town.

Lookout Mountain, Golden.

Probably the most popular local site, it does have a very restricted landing zone (not the place for beginners!). The site has complex rules regarding it's use and pilots are encouraged to contact the Rocky Mountain Hang Gliding Association before using it.

The Landing Zone is a quarter mile on the right past the junction of Hwy. 93 and Clear Creek Canyon (Hwy. 6).

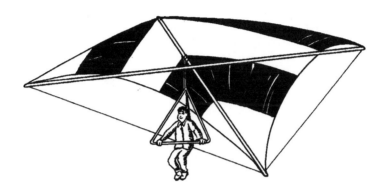

An early hang glider design, pilot in sitting position

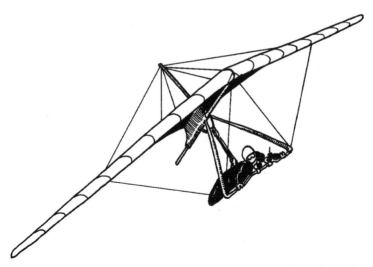

A modern hang glider. The wing is now double-skinned and has bracing wires. Pilot now flies in the prone position inside a warm and streamline bag

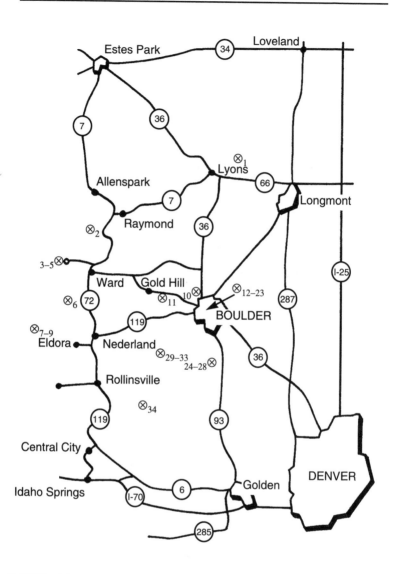

1:	Rabbit Mountain	
2:	Peaceful Valley Loop	
3:	Mount Audobon	
4:	Blue Lake & Mt. Toll	
5:	Jean Lunning Scenic Trail	
6:	Sourdough Trail	
7:	Diamond Lake	
8:	Devils Thumb Pass	
9:	Eldora to Caribou Trail	
10:	Mt. Sanitas & Dakota Ridge	
11:	Bald Mountain	
12:	Boulder Creek	
13:	East Boulder Trail	
14:	South Boulder Trail	
15:	Tenderfoot Trail	
16:	Ute & Rangeview Trails	
17:	McClintock Trail	
18:	Enchanted Mesa Trail	
19:	Mesa Trail	
20:	Green Mountain	
21:	Bear Peak	
22:	Royal Arch	
23:	Walter Orr Roberts Trail	
24:	Community Ditch	
25:	Doudy Draw Trail	
26:	Fowler Trail	
27:	Rattlesnake Gulch	
28:	Eldorado Canyon	
29:	Meyers Homestead	
30:	Columbine Gulch	
31:	Crescent Meadows	
32:	South Boulder Creek Trail	
33:	Walker Ranch Loop	
34:	Frazer Meadow Loop	

Hiking

The Boulder area is rich in hiking trails and this section can only touch the surface of what is available. We have listed some of the best trails and concentrated on those that allow a loop trail as opposed to an "out-and-back".

For the trails near town, sneakers are generally adequate footwear, whilst hiking boots or sturdy walking shoes will be preferable on the rugged trails in the mountains.

We strongly advise the use of a map and compass, particularly in the mountains, as they can not only assist in getting around, but are also helpful in identifying distant peaks and features. It's also fun at the end of the day to trace your route and perhaps lay future plans.

A note regarding these trails during the winter months. Some of the high trails may be impassable during the winter and spring due to high snow drifts. The time required may well differ from the times given here for these and unforeseen reasons.

When in the high mountains, be aware that thunderstorms roll through fairly regularly in the early afternoon. Try to be off summits and exposed ridges by this time. For this reason, an early start is worth considering.

Finally, if you have exhausted all the hiking trails in this chapter and still hunger for more, why not try some of the trails listed in the Cross-Country Skiing Section? During the summer months these are fine trails in their own right, and will offer the solitude that many of the low level trails will lack. The same can also be said of many of the Mountain Biking trails.

Rabbit Mountain

Distance: 3½ miles of trails
Difficulty: Easy
Terrain: Dirt track
Time Required: Half day
Start elevation: 5,400' **Elevation gain:** 660'

Rabbit Mountain offers a different perspective on the plains and foothills. It is also an excellent viewpoint for Longs Peak (14,255').

Take Hwy. 36 from Boulder north to Lyons. At the junction with Hwy. 66, turn right and then left soon after (at the orange water tank) on 53rd which leads onto N. 55th Street. Trailhead is a short distance further north, about 4 miles from Hwy. 66.

Trail heads east and up onto a saddle where a dirt track leads off to the left. This rather rocky trail leads to the Little Thompson Overlook. Just after the junction for the Little Thompson Overlook, a road branches off to the right. Along here - about a 1/2 mile - there is a track leading off to the right. This - the Eagle Wind Trail - follows the ridge for a short distance.

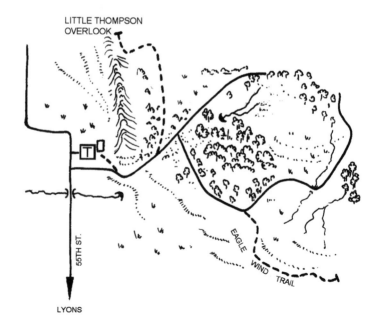

LITTLE THOMPSON
OVERLOOK

55TH ST.

EAGLE WIND TRAIL

LYONS

Peaceful Valley Loop

Distance: 8½ miles round trip
Difficulty: Difficult & Strenuous
Terrain: Dirt track & Jeep trail
Time Required: All day
Start elevation: 8,638' **Elevation gain:** 1,182'

Snow drifts may block the trail, particularly the second half, through late June, and puddles also form on the road and can be deceptively deep. Nonetheless, a fine trail.

Trailhead is at at Camp Dick which is on Colorado Road 92 just off Hwy. 72 (Peak to Peak Highway) at Peaceful Valley.

The trail heads west following Middle St. Vrain road for about 3.5 miles to an obvious signed junction. The jeep trail continues on here to Red Deer Lake. Take a left here - Road #507 - and head uphill along a narrower trail. This joins Road #961 after ½ mile. Trail then heads back east, bordering Beaver Reservoir to join the Sourdough Trail. Take a left and head downhill back to the trailhead.

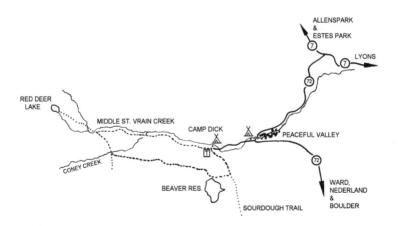

Mount Audobon

Distance: 3½ miles one way
Difficulty: Moderate
Terrain: Dirt trail
Time Required: Full day
Start elevation: 10,480' **Elevation gain: 2,743'**

A summer season trail.

Trail starts from the Mitchell Lake Trailhead at Brainard Lake. From Nederland, take Hwy. 72 north to Ward. Just past Ward take the left turn sign posted for Brainard Lake. Follow this road past Brainard Lake. The trailhead is off to the right.

Trail is well marked from the trailhead. After an hour, the trail forks left, leaving what is essentially the Buchanan Pass Trail, and the the gradient then increases. The middle section of the trail is perhaps the least interesting. Keep going, past a small area of snow - sometimes red due to algae growth - and after several 'false summits', it's a relief to reach the rocky summit ridge. From here, head south towards the summit for excellent views in all directions. There are shelters from the wind on the summit. Take care to be off the summit by early afternoon to avoid the '2 o'clock thunderstorms'.

Bighorn Sheep

NIWOT RIDGE   SHOSHONI PEAK 12,967'   PAWNEE PEAK 12,943'   MT. AUDOBON 13,223'

NAVAJO PEAK 13,409'   POINT 12,878'   MT. TOLL 12,979'

APACHE PEAK 13,441'

The Indian Peaks from Brainard Lake

ue Lake & Mt. Toll

niles one way

oderate to Blue Lake. Difficult up to Mt. Toll

rt trail, talus and talus up to Mt. Toll

Time Required: full day

Start elevation: 10,480' **Elevation gain:** 820' (2,500')

Trail starts from the Mitchell Lake Trailhead at Brainard Lake. From Nederland, take Hwy. 72 north to Ward. Just past Ward take the left turn sign posted for Brainard Lake. Follow this road past Brainard Lake. The trailhead is off to the right.

Trail heads north-west from trailhead up past Mitchell Lake and on up to Blue Lake. Blue Lake is well named and in early summer may still contain ice floes. If you have some surplus energy, walk around the lake and then up the left shoulder for the last ½ mile to the summit of Mt. Toll. The views across the Continental Divide are stunning.

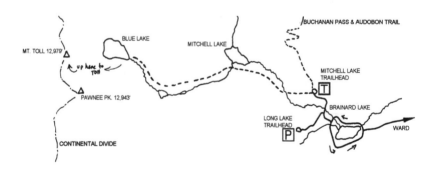

Mt. Toll from Blue Lake. The trail up to the top goes up the snow slope on the left side of the peak

Jean Lunning Scenic Trail

Distance: 3 miles round trip
Difficulty: Easy
Terrain: Dirt trail
Time Required: Half day
Start elevation: 10,520' **Elevation gain:** 40'

    Trail starts from the Long Lake Trailhead at Brainard Lake. From Nederland, take Hwy. 72 north to Ward. Just past Ward take the left turn sign posted for Brainard Lake. Follow this road past Brainard Lake. The trailhead is off to the right.
    From the trailhead, head west through the trees for several hundred yards. At an obvious clearing, noted for its' mosquito colony, cross the St. Vrain Creek using the bridge. The trail then trends right to the edge of the lake before heading back into the trees to follow a course paralleling the lake shore. After crossing several streams, the trail turns to the north, crosses back over the creek and rejoins the Long Lake Trail. Turn right and follow this wide, accommodating trail back to the trailhead.

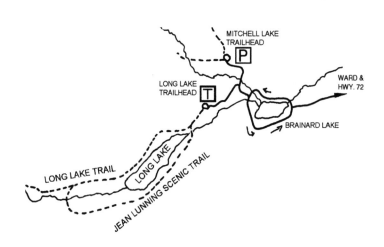

Sourdough Trail

Distance: 6 miles one way
Difficulty: Difficult
Terrain: Narrow path with rocks and tree roots
Time Required: Full day
Start elevation: 9,200'   **Elevation gain:** 1,040'

The Sourdough Trail is a scenic walk, mainly through trees with occasional views of the plains and mountains.

Trail starts on CR. 116 which is off Hwy. 72, 7 miles north of Nederland towards Ward. CR. 116 is sign posted for the University of Colorado Mountain Research Station. Drive along 116 for about ¼ mile to the signs for the trail. There is limited parking here.

The trail heads north, contouring the east side of Niwot Mountain. It is also a Cross Country ski trail and has been marked by hammering blue diamonds into trees along the route. The length of the hike is really up to you, and can even be started from the Red Rocks trailhead on the Brainard Lake Road.

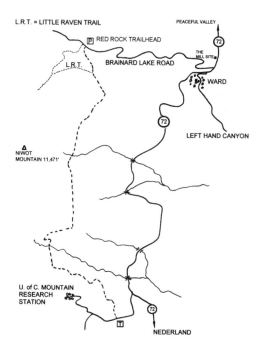

Diamond Lake

Distance: 2 miles one way
Difficulty: Easy
Terrain: Dirt trail
Time Required: Half day
Start elevation: 10,120' **Elevation gain:** 800'

From Nederland, drive south on Hwy. 72 for a short distance before taking a right towards Eldora. Drive through Eldora and continue on the jeep trail to the Fourth of July Trailhead. This is a fairly rough road but can be managed by most vehicles.

Hike north west on the Arapahoe Pass Trail for a short distance. Then break off left downhill to cross the North Fork of Middle Boulder Creek. Ascend the wooded hillside and continue on and around to emerge at the lake.

Devils Thumb Pass

Distance: 5 miles one way
Difficulty: Difficult
Terrain: Dirt trail
Time Required: Full day
Start elevation: 9,010'   **Elevation gain:** 2,737'

Great views across the Continental Divide.

From Nederland, drive south on Hwy. 72 for a short distance before taking a right towards Eldora. Drive through Eldora and continue for a short stretch to a junction by a sign. There is limited parking here and some just before the junction.

Trail is well signposted. Take the left at the junction towards Hessie. The trail follows the Middle Boulder Creek initially, then Jasper Creek which leads up to Jasper Lake. Devils Thumb Lake lies another ¾ mile further on. For those with more energy, the walk up to the Pass is recommended. From the lake, head south-west ascending to a small, unnamed lake and then climb steeply up the hillside to the south, then south-west up onto the col. Note: Don't try to follow the direct trail marked on some maps, as it doesn't exist.

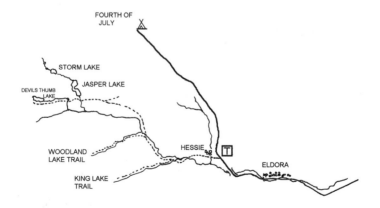

Eldora To Caribou Trail

Distance: 6 miles one way
Difficulty: Difficult
Terrain: Jeep trail
Time Required: Full day
Start elevation: 8,750' **Elevation gain:** 1,490'

Attractions include the ghost town of Caribou and evidence of a bygone era.

From Nederland, drive south on Hwy. 72 for a short distance before taking a right towards Eldora. The trail starts from Washington Street on the west side of town - just off Huron Street. Parking is limited.

Follow the jeep trail as it heads initially east, climbing the side of Eldorado Mountain and then heads back northwest. After about 4 miles, the gradient eases as you arrive at Caribou Flats. Continue north then down to the old silver mining town site of Caribou. This is now a quiet meadow, but was once a booming town of 3,000 people. Silver is still mined here by the Hendricks Mining Company.

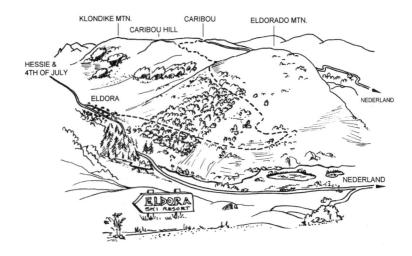

Mt. Sanitas & Dakota Ridge

Distance: 3 miles round trip
Difficulty: Moderate
Terrain: Dirt trail, steep in places
Time Required: Half Day
Start elevation: 5,550'   **Elevation gain:** 1,200'

    The Mt Sanitas area is a popular one with climbers out for an evening's bouldering, runners, hikers and dog-walkers. Sadly, until the dog-walkers start picking up the mess their pooches make, this area will tend to have a distinct odor in warm weather. Bags for this purpose are available at the trailhead.

    Starts at the parking lot at the end of Mapleton Avenue just past the Mapleton Center on the right.

    From the picnic area, head north on a well maintained trail then cross a ditch and trend north-west up the obvious ridge of Mt. Sanitas to the summit. From there, head down to the north-east into the valley between Mt. Sanitas and the Dakota Ridge. Climb back up onto the Dakota Ridge and follow this back to the trailhead, or if short of time, follow the valley back to the trailhead.

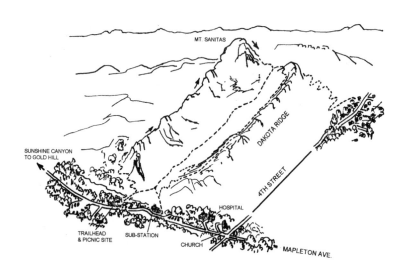

Bald Mountain

Distance: One mile round trip
Difficulty: Easy
Terrain: Maintained footpath
Time Required: Not a lot
Start elevation: 6,400'   **Elevation gain:** 760'

The main attraction of Bald Mountain lies more in its easy access than any other intrinsic qualities. Good views of the cunningly camouflaged Boulder Filtration Plant.

Bald Mountain lies on Sunshine Canyon Drive, about 5 miles west of downtown Boulder. Take Mapleton Avenue which becomes Sunshine Canyon. The trailhead is on the left.

The trail loops around to the top of Bald Mountain. It is well marked and maintained. The summit is exposed and can be unpleasant in windy weather.

The Raccoon
Favors woodland and forest and occasionally, the odd dumpster

Boulder Creek

Distance: 7 miles one way
Difficulty: Easy
Terrain: Concrete Path - wheelchair accessible
Time Required: Not a lot

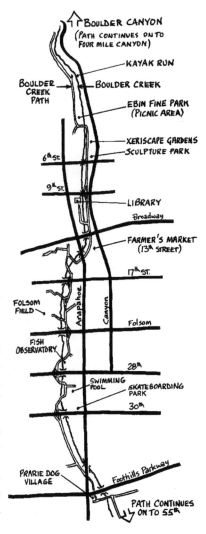

Renowned throughout the area, the Creek Path can be an idyllic amble through a range of habitats, or, on a bad day, a heart stopping gamble as a few mindless morons attached to various sized wheels use it as a race track.

Attractions along the way include a kayak slalom course (at its best during the Spring runoff), sculpture park and fish observatory, and the Cottonwood Grove and Cottonwood Ponds at the east end of the trail offer a habitat to a wide variety of birds and mammals.

Runs from the east side of 55th Street, near the junction with Valmont, to end at the junction of Boulder Canyon and Four Mile Canyon. Access to the path is possible at numerous points along its route.

The trail follows the Boulder Creek up into the Foothills. It is well maintained and signed.

East Boulder Trail

Distance: 7 miles one way
Difficulty: Easy
Terrain: Dirt road / track
Time Required: Not a lot

A very popular trail for runners, hikers and cyclists. Bird watching is popular at the Teller Lakes.

The trail starts at the Teller Farm Trailhead located on Arapahoe Avenue, 1 mile east of 75th Street.

The trail goes north on dirt road until Valmont Drive. At Valmont the trail continues north just west of the intersection. Follow the trail up to where it meets the Gunbarrel Trail. Turn west on the Gunbarrel Trail and follow up onto the Mesa. The Trail ends at 75th and Lookout Road.

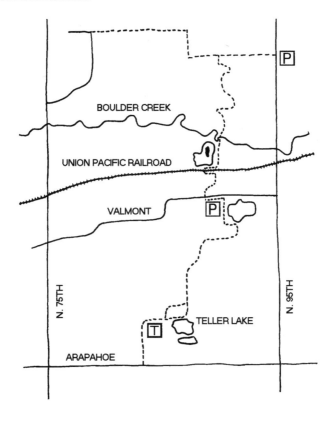

South Boulder Trail

Distance: 3 miles one way
Difficulty: Easy
Terrain: Dirt trail
Time Required: Not a lot

Interesting wetland habitat with a wide variety of birds. Short, self-guided nature trail for the first section.

Starts at the Bobolink Trailhead on Baseline Road just west of Cherryvale Road.

This largely level trail heads south along the creek, to a slight detour for an underpass under South Boulder Road. Head back west to re-join the trail. The trail ends abruptly at a small lake outside Marshall. There is no public access to the lake. The mid-section of the trail by the South Boulder Road can become very muddy during the Spring.

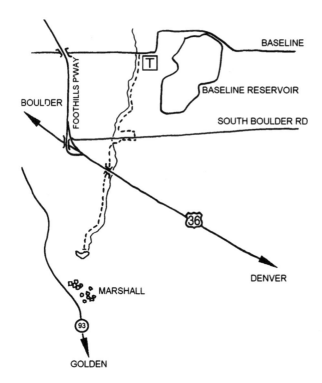

Tenderfoot Trail

Distance: 2¼ miles round trip
Difficulty: Moderate
Terrain: Narrow dirt trail and fire road
Time Required: Not a lot

An attractive trail which gives good views of the Indian Peaks to the west.

Take Baseline west and then on up Flagstaff Mountain. The trail starts from the Realization Point Parking lot.

From the trailhead, walk past the picnic tables then take the Tenderfoot Trail where it leads gently downhill. The trail continues along the side of the hill to a junction. A short spur leads straight on to a small peak which offers views west. Follow the signed Tenderfoot Trail down to the left, and after a short while, it meets Chapman Drive Fire Road. From here head back uphill to meet the Flagstaff Road just west of the start.

Steller's Jay
Black crest, with vivid blue wings and tail. Common in the Foothills. Lives on insects and seeds.

Ute Trail & Rangeview Trail

Distance: 1¼ miles round trip
Difficulty: Easy
Terrain: Dirt trail
Time Required: Not a lot

    Take Baseline west and then on up Flagstaff Mountain. The trail starts from the Realization Point Parking lot.

    From the parking lot, take the Ute Trail which starts from just beyond the sign and heads uphill. The trail is fairly steep at the beginning, but soon levels out as it approaches the top of the hill. Just before the picnic area at the top, Rangeview Trail heads west at a four way junction. Follow this as it swings around to the south, through a series of switchbacks to end at Realization Point.

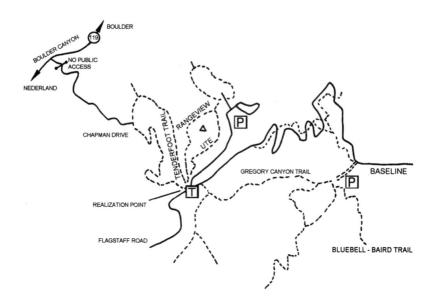

McClintock Nature Trail

Distance: ¾ mile one way
Difficulty: Easy
Terrain: Narrow dirt trail, steep in places
Time Required: Not a lot

A popular self guided nature trail.

Starts from behind the Chautauqua Auditorium, beside the picnic shelter. Chautauqua Park is on Baseline and 9th, just before Flagstaff Mountain.

The trail, which is narrow and steeply stepped in places, follows a shaded route up the hillside. It ends on (or can be started from) the Mesa Trail.

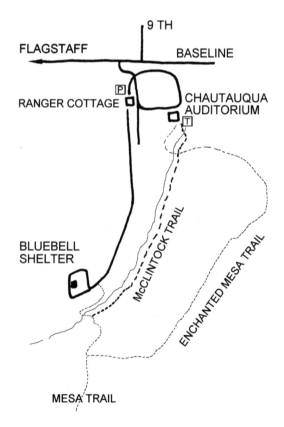

Enchanted Mesa Trail

Distance: 1½ miles one way
Difficulty: Easy
Terrain: Dirt road
Time Required: Not a lot

Starts from behind the Chautauqua Auditorium, beside the picnic shelter. Chautauqua Park is on Baseline and 9th, just before Flagstaff Mountain.

Trail follows the Fire Road up past the reservoir structure and then on through the trees to join the Mesa Trail. Can be combined with the McClintock Nature Trail for a satisfying loop trail.

See map on previous page.

The Flatirons
Much loved symbol of Boulder, the Flatirons are formed of the 270 million year old sandstones and conglomerates of the Fountain Formation.

Mesa Trail

Distance: 6¼ miles one way
Difficulty: Easy
Terrain: Dirt trail
Time Required: Half day

A Boulder favorite, the Mesa Trail follows along the edge of the Flatirons, giving a good perspective of the rock formations. We counted 26 pinnacles along here. You may spot more.

Starts from Ranger Cottage at Chautauqua Park. Chautauqua Park is on Baseline and 9th, just before Flagstaff Mountain.

Follow the Bluebell road south to the restrooms just before the Bluebell Shelter. The Mesa Trail proper starts from just to the left of the restrooms. Trail then meanders south along the edge of the Foothills, to meet the Eldorado Canyon Road - Hwy. 170 - at the South Mesa Trailhead. Trail is well signed.

Colorado Marble 1½"-2"

Colorado Anglewing 2"

Edwards Fritillary 2½"

 *Colorado Hairstreak 1½"*

Some of the butterflies that may be seen in the Boulder area

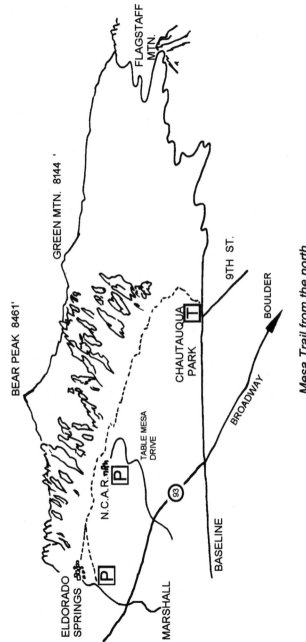

FLAGSTAFF MTN.

GREEN MTN. 8144 '

BEAR PEAK 8461'

9TH ST.

CHAUTAUQUA PARK

T

BOULDER

Mesa Trail from the north

TABLE MESA DRIVE

P

N.C.A.R.

BROADWAY

93

ELDORADO SPRINGS

P

MARSHALL

BASELINE

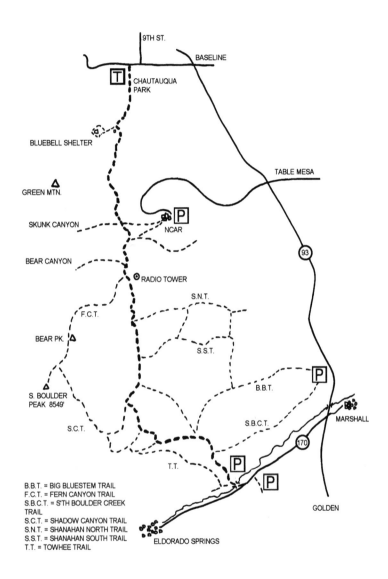

9TH ST.

BASELINE

T CHAUTAUQUA PARK

BLUEBELL SHELTER

TABLE MESA

GREEN MTN.

SKUNK CANYON

P

NCAR

93

BEAR CANYON

RADIO TOWER

S.N.T.

F.C.T.

BEAR PK.

S.S.T.

S. BOULDER PEAK 8549'

P

B.B.T.

S.B.C.T.

MARSHALL

S.C.T.

170

T.T.

P

P

GOLDEN

B.B.T. = BIG BLUESTEM TRAIL
F.C.T. = FERN CANYON TRAIL
S.B.C.T. = S'TH BOULDER CREEK TRAIL
S.C.T. = SHADOW CANYON TRAIL
S.N.T. = SHANAHAN NORTH TRAIL
S.S.T. = SHANAHAN SOUTH TRAIL
T.T. = TOWHEE TRAIL

ELDORADO SPRINGS

Plan of the Mesa Trail, showing interconnecting trails

Green Mountain

Distance: 5½ miles round trip
Difficulty: Moderate
Terrain: Narrow dirt trail
Time Required: Half day
Start elevation: 5,760' **Elevation gain:** 2,384'

Large sections of the trail are in woodland, with occasional good views of Boulder.

Starts at the Gregory Canyon Trailhead, just off Baseline, at the foot of Flagstaff Mountain.

This well -signed trail follows the Gregory Canyon Trail initially from the Trailhead. This loops around to meet the Ranger Trail at Green Mountain Lodge (restrooms). The Ranger Trail is then followed - with some exposure - past a junction with the H.L. Greenman Trail (if short of time, the trail can be cut by taking this spur to join the Saddle Rock Trail back to the trailhead) .Follow the Greenman Trail to another junction, this time with the Green Mountain West Ridge Trail, turn east on this and on up to the summit of Green Mountain (8,144'). From the tree-crowded summit, descend using the H.L.Greenman Trail to where the Saddle Rock Trail begins, then follow this back to trailhead.

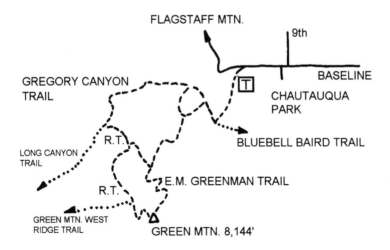

Bear Peak

Distance: 2½ miles one way
Difficulty: Moderate
Terrain: Dirt trail
Time Required: Half day
Start elevation: 6,080' **Elevation gain:** 2,381'

An impressive summit climb that well justifies the effort.

Start at parking lot at NCAR. To get to NCAR, take Broadway south out of town. Turn right at Table Mesa and follow the road up to the Center. The self-guided tour of NCAR is interesting if time permits.

Trail initially follows the short Walter Orr Roberts Trail which starts from the west side of the NCAR buildings. The trail then heads down to the left at a noticeboard, to a saddle, then climbs up to the Water Tower on the ridge. Passing the Water Tower, the Mesa Trail is joined and followed south for a short distance. Pass the entrance to Bear Canyon, and then at a junction, take the Fern Canyon Trail south-west and uphill. The Fern Canyon Trail leads to the summit. To return, retrace your steps.

Shortish detour: just after you join the Mesa Trail, a trail leads off west to Mallory Cave, Boulder's best known cave. This leads steeply up the hillside for about ½ mile to the cave.

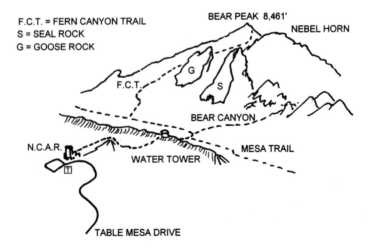

Royal Arch

Distance: 2 miles one way
Difficulty: Moderate
Terrain: Steep narrow trail
Time Required: Not a lot
Start elevation: 5,680'   **Elevation gain:** 1,000'

Royal Arch is a 20' high natural arch created by erosion and faulting. Great views also of the city.

Starts from Ranger Cottage at Chautauqua Park. Chautauqua Park is on Baseline and 9th, just before Flagstaff Mtn.

Take the Bluebell Road up past the restrooms to the Bluebell Shelter (½ mile) and then fork left at the shelter.The Arch Trail is marked with a small sign. The trail gains height through a series of switchbacks then up through thick woodland. An outcrop of rock is passed, a short descent then leads to another series of switchbacks up to another rock outcrop. The Arch is here although it may not be possible to see it until you are under it. The best photographic view point is just south of the Arch on a short outcrop of rock. Be aware that there is a steep drop just here - best to ignore any 'back-a-bit' type photographic suggestions.

The Royal Arch

Walter Orr Roberts Nature Trail

Distance: ½ mile round trip
Difficulty: Easy
Terrain: Level gravel trail. Wheelchair accessible
Time Required: Not a lot

An interesting self-guided nature trail. Its short length and easy accessibility from town make it a popular outing. The self-guided tour of NCAR (National Center for Atmospheric Research) is worth doing if time permits. (TIP: The cafe in the NCAR building is open to the public and is very pleasant).

Start at parking lot at NCAR. To get to there, take Broadway south out of town Turn right on Table Mesa and follow the road up to the Center.

Trail loops around the top of the small ridge on which NCAR rests. It is well signed and maintained.

NCAR from the Walter Orr Roberts Nature Trail

Community Ditch

Distance: 5 miles one way
Difficulty: Easy
Terrain: Dirt trail
Time Required: Not a lot

An attractive trail, particularly in the early summer when the ditch is full and so are the flowers.

Trail starts at Doudy Draw Trail Head on south side of Hwy. 170, the Eldorado Canyon Road, 1½ miles west of Hwy. 93.

Take the trail south to picnic area and restrooms then head east on the Community Ditch Trail which is followed until the junction with Hwy. 93. Cross Hwy. 93 and continue along the trail almost to Marshall Reservoir. The trail avoids the Reservoir - no public access - and then zig-zags down to the Marshall Mesa Trailhead.

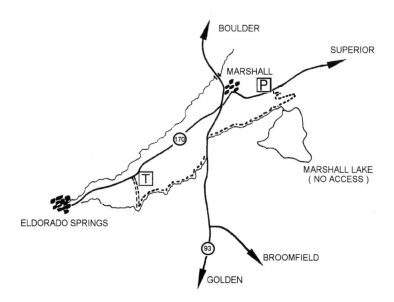

Doudy Draw Trail

Distance: 5 miles round trip
Difficulty: Easy
Terrain: Dirt trail
Time Required: Half day
Start elevation: 5,640'   **Elevation gain:** 400'

Trail starts at Doudy Draw Trailhead on south side of Hwy. 170, the Eldorado Canyon Road, 1½ miles west of Hwy. 93.

Amble south from trailhead, past restrooms following the gully (the 'Draw') up to a left turn which takes the trail out of the gully and up onto the mesa. At the Flatirons Vista Trailhead, cross the highway and follow it north towards Boulder for a short stretch to access the Greenbelt Plateau Trailhead which is on the far side of the Broomfield Road. From there, take the trail north and down to where it meets the Community Ditch Trail and then follow this west, across Hwy. 93 and back to the trailhead.

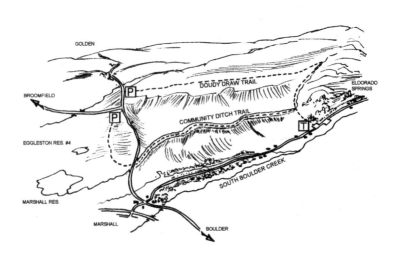

Fowler Trail

Distance: ¼ mile
Difficulty: Easy
Terrain: Level path. Wheelchair accessible
Time Required: Not a lot

Good viewpoint for watching climbers on Redgarden Wall and the Bastille. Also views of the town of Eldorado Springs.

Trail is inside Eldorado Canyon State Park. Take Hwy. 93 south out of Boulder, turn right at junction for Eldorado Springs (Hwy. 170) some 5 miles from downtown. Drive through Eldorado Springs and enter the park. A fee is required, currently $3 per vehicle. The nearest parking to the start of the trail is about ½ mile further on.

Trail goes east from the noticeboard which gives details on both this trail and Rattlesnake Gulch Trail.

View down Eldorado Canyon from the Fowler Trail. The Naked Edge is the knife edge on the left, the smaller block on the right is the Bastille

Rattlesnake Gulch

Distance: 2¼ miles one way
Difficulty: Difficult
Terrain: Narrow, steep trail
Time Required: Half day
Start elevation: 5,680'   **Elevation gain:** 1,680'

An interesting hike which takes you to a commanding position above the canyon.

This trail is inside the Eldorado Canyon State Park. Take Hwy. 93 south out of Boulder, turn right at junction for Eldorado Springs (Hwy. 170) some 5 miles from downtown. Drive through Eldorado Springs and enter the park. A fee is required, currently $3 per vehicle. The nearest parking to the start of the trail is about ½ mile further on.

Trail follows the Fowler Trail initially, then forks right and winds its way up the hillside. At about the halfway point the ruins of the old Crags Hotel are reached. The trail becomes narrower from here as it climbs up to the left to meet the Denver & Rio Grande Western Railroad which is still in use. For trail map, see the page 171.

The view from the top of Rattlesnake Gulch Trail. Redgarden Wall in the middle distance and Boulder in the far distance

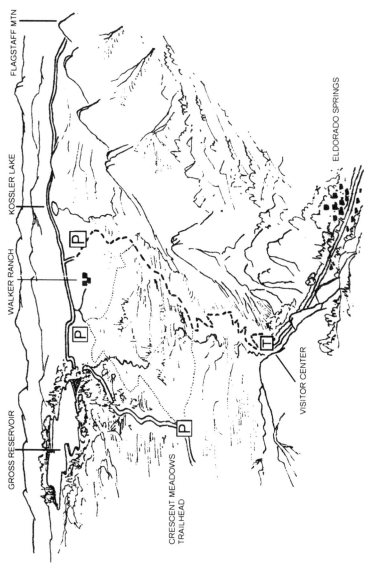

The Eldorado Canyon Trail

Eldorado Canyon Trail

Distance: 5 miles one way
Difficulty: Difficult
Terrain: Narrow, steep trail
Time Required: Full day
Start elevation: 5,680'   **Elevation gain:** 1,000'

One of the best trails in the Boulder area.

Trail is inside Eldorado Canyon State Park. Take Hwy. 93 south out of Boulder, turn right at junction for Eldorado Springs (Hwy. 170) some 5 miles from downtown. Drive through Eldorado Springs and enter the park. A fee is required, currently $3 per vehicle. Follow the road through to the park, over the creek and either park on the right just beyond the bridge, or take a left down to the Visitor Center.

Trail heads north up the steep slope, then contours around to the west before a steep descent down to a junction with the Crescent Meadows Trail near the South Boulder Creek. Keep right and follow the trail as it heads gradually uphill and to the north to the Upper Eldorado Canyon Trailhead on Bison Road.

For trail map, see previous page.

Peregrine Falcon

Meyers Homestead Trail

Distance: 2½ miles one way
Difficulty: Easy
Terrain: Dirt trail
Time Required: Not a lot
Start elevation: 7,440' **Elevation gain:** 455'

A pleasant amble through meadows past an old homestead site. Great views towards the mountains from the overlook at the trail end.

Trail is on the Walker Ranch. From Boulder, take Baseline up over Flagstaff and on past Kossler Lake. Walker Ranch is about 5 miles out of town. Starts at the Trailhead and group picnic area on the right, just before the left turn to the Walker Ranch Historic Site.

Trail is a gentle walk on a wide trail through meadows and ends at a scenic overlook.

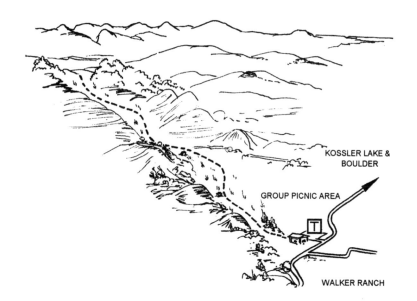

KOSSLER LAKE &
BOULDER

GROUP PICNIC AREA

WALKER RANCH

Columbine Gulch Trail

Distance: 1½ miles one way
Difficulty: Moderate
Terrain: Narrow trail
Time Required: Not a lot
Start elevation: 6,700'   **Elevation gain:** -648'

One of the finest trails on the Walker Ranch site, it is less well travelled than the other main trails, and can be particularly pleasant in the Spring when the flowers are in bloom.

Trail starts at the South Boulder Creek Trailhead. From Boulder, take Baseline up over Flagstaff and on past Kossler Lake. Walker Ranch is about 5 miles out of town. Just past the group picnic area on the right and where the road does a sharp right, a stony road goes off and down to the left. Follow this for a short distance to the trailhead.

The trail heads east from the trailhead. Taking a winding path across the hillside before entering dense woodland and then descending through a series of switchbacks to end on the Eldorado Canyon Trail.

Crescent Meadows Trail

Distance: 1¾ miles one way
Difficulty: Difficult
Terrain: Narrow dirt trail
Time Required: Not a lot
Start elevation: 6,700'   **Elevation gain:** -696'

A popular trail, it starts with a gentle stroll across the meadows with dramatic views towards Eldorado Canyon, before descending steeply down to the South Boulder Creek.

The trail involves some steep sections where care should be exercised and the final steep descent down to the creek is very loose. The creek is crossed via a footbridge before joining the Eldorado Canyon Trail.

Trail starts form the Crescent Meadows trailhead which is on the Gross Reservoir to Copperdale road. From Boulder, take Baseline up over Flagstaff and on past Kossler Lake. Walker Ranch is about 5 miles out of town. Drive past the group picnic area on the right and follow the road round a sharp right. Take the next left turn, about a mile further on. Follow the stony road as it descends down to the South Boulder Creek and then climbs back up to the Crescent Meadows Parking lot on the left.

From the trailhead, the trail heads east across the meadows. The trail is obvious and not difficult to follow.

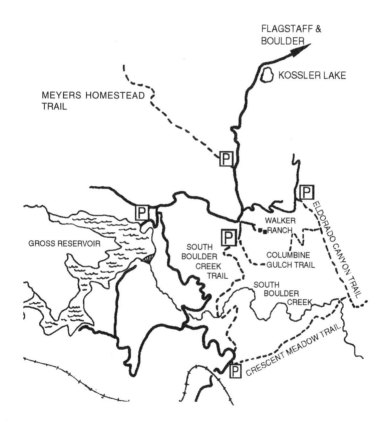

Walker Ranch - main trails, and Gross Reservoir

South Boulder Creek Trail

Distance: 2¾ miles one way
Difficulty: Moderate
Terrain: Dirt trail
Time Required: Not a lot
Start elevation: 6,700'   **Elevation gain:** -584'

A wide, open trail, it passes several rocky outcrops as it descends down to the creek. There are several pleasant picnic areas by the creek

Trail starts at the South Boulder Creek Trailhead. From Boulder, take Baseline up over Flagstaff and on past Kossler Lake. Walker Ranch is about 5 miles out of town. Just past the group picnic area on the right and where the road does a sharp right, a stony road goes off and down to the left. Follow this for a short distance to the trailhead.

From the trailhead, head south following an old fire road down to the creek, then steeply up to join the Gross Reservoir Road, just north of the parking lot for the Crescent Meadows Trail.

Walker Ranch Loop Trail

Distance: 8 miles round trip
Difficulty: Difficult
Terrain: Narrow trails, steep in places
Time Required: Full day
Start elevation: 6,700'   **Elevation gain:** 400'

A popular mountain biking circuit, the Walker Ranch trail links the three previous trails together to give a satisfying day out. It has a remote feeling which can be enhanced by avoiding weekends and holidays. Can be done in either direction with the South Boulder Creek Trailhead being probably the best starting point.

BEAVER   RACCOON   BOBCAT   BADGER

DEER   RABBIT   SQUIRREL   HUMAN

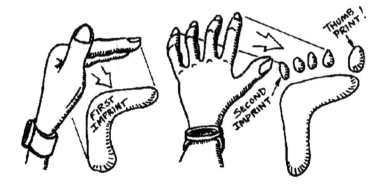

Tracks in the snow

Golden Gate Canyon State Park

The Golden Gate Canyon State Park covers an area of more than 10,000 acres, 7,000 of which is backcountry. Despite its location close to Denver, it is surprisingly under utilized and often seems to be empty except for groups at picnic spots and fishing at the park ponds. The backcountry trails are usually deserted and this makes the park particularly attractive for those looking for a more remote backcountry day out. It is well served by three campgrounds and numerous backcountry campsites. These backcountry sites are basic but, even in summer when the campgrounds are full to capacity, they may well be empty. For more information on camping in the park, check the Camping Section.

Entry Fee for park is $3 per vehicle. Pass is valid until noon the following day.

Frazer Meadow Loop

Distance: 4½ miles round trip
Difficulty: Difficult
Terrain: Narrow & rocky trail
Time Required: Half day
Start elevation: 8,600' **Elevation gain:** 850'

From Nederland, head south on Hwy. 72, then where Hwy. 72 cuts back east towards Coal Creek, continue on Hwy. 119 towards Central City until a sign off to the left leads to the Golden Gate Canyon State Park. Follow this road to a unmanned park pay station then take a right and follow the road into the park. The trailhead - Ole' Barn Knoll Picnic Area - is on the right about 1½ miles further on.

From the picnic area, head away from the road down to the creek to join the Elk Trail. At the junction, take a left and follow the trail as it parallels the road. After a short distance, the trail crosses the road then heads up the hillside. This section of the trail is part of the Mule Deer Trail. Ignore the three trails going off right and continue through the aspens and meadow to the log cabins at Frazer Meadows. (Judging by the size of the roof timbers, and their condition, it may be wise to stay out). From the cabins continue north for a short stretch before taking the Coyote Trail off to the left. Follow this gently up to the ridge.There is a short steep section to get down off the ridge, then the trail zigzags back down to the road. Cross the road and creek and then at the Elk Trail junction turn left and head back to where you started.

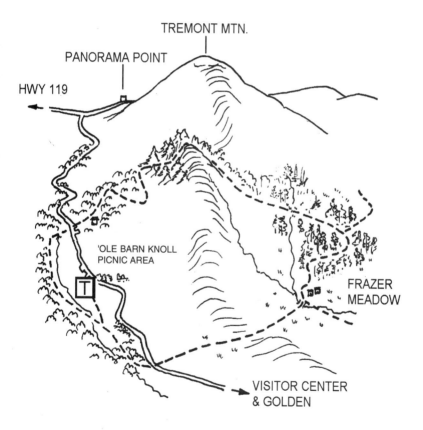

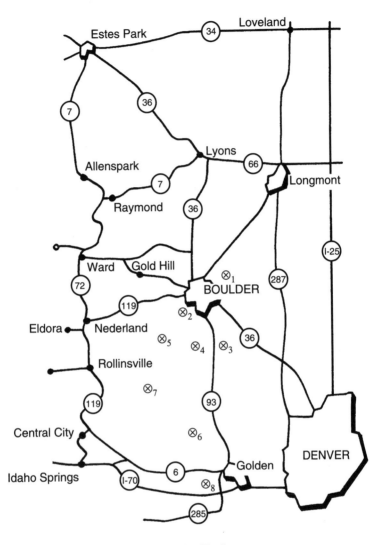

1:     East Boulder Trail
2:     Mesa Trail
3:     Marshall Mesa and Doudy Draw
4:     Eldorado Canyon Trail
5:     Walker Ranch
6:     White Ranch
7:     Golden Gate Canyon State Park
8:     Apex Park

Horseback Riding

Colorado has been called Horse Country. Horses seem to thrive in the high prairie climate. The year round sunshine helps keep the trails open much of the year. This is only one reason why Boulder County has the one of the largest horse ownership per capita in the USA.

Other reasons include there is still enough land to ride on, many local breeding farms and boarding stables, numerous events, clubs and shows.

In this region, the Boulder County Horsemen's Association represents the horseriders in legal, access and general matters. It is also a useful contact for riding in the area. They also educate riders and hold seminars. The President of the Association - Creighton Stewart - can be contacted at (303) 776-9568.

The open spaces around Boulder offer many riding opportunities to the horse man and woman. The higher trails in the mountains should be treated with respect as bad weather can occur at any time. Protective rainwear is worth taking when venturing in to the wild.

Horse rental is available in the area and we list some outfits in Reference 3.

Note to other trail users:

A horses natural instinct when frightened is to flee. This is a dominating characteristic, as the horse is prey, not a predator. For this reason, please respect the horse and rider if you meet them on the trail.

Suggested rides in the area

East Boulder Trail

The trail starts at the Teller Farm Trailhead located on Arapahoe Avenue, 1 mile east of 75th Street. A mainly level trail on dirt road and track, about 7 miles one way.

Mesa Trail

Starts from Ranger Cottage at Chautauqua Park. Chautauqua Park is on Baseline and 9th, just before Flagstaff Mountain. A fine trail winding its way along the foot of the Flatirons. About 6.2 miles from the Park down to Eldorado Springs.

Marshall Mesa & Doudy Draw

A series of trails interconnect in this area around Marshall and Eldorado Springs offering a number of variations.

Eldorado Canyon Trail

Trail is inside Eldorado Canyon State Park. Take Hwy. 93 south out of Boulder, turn right at junction for Eldorado Springs (Hwy. 170) some 5 miles from downtown. Drive through Eldorado Springs and enter the park. A fee is required, currently $3 per vehicle. Follow the road through to the park, over the creek and either park on the right just beyond the bridge, or take a left down to the Visitor Center.

The trail heads, sometimes steeply, up to the Walker Ranch. About 5 miles one way.

Walker Ranch

Walker Ranch is located about 9 miles out of Boulder on the Flagstaff Mountain Road. The Ranch contains a network of trails ranging in difficulty.

White Ranch

Located northwest of Golden, White Ranch offers superb riding in a remote location. The nearest trailhead from Boulder is 17 miles out of Boulder on Hwy. 93. The ranch is sign posted off to the right - W. 56th Street. The trail head is 1½ miles further on. There are numerous trails, and trail maps are available at the trailhead.

Golden Gate Canyon State Park

Horseback riding is allowed within the park and the Rimrock

Loop at Aspen Meadows Campground has campgrounds and parking designed for horseback riders. The remote Deer Creek campsites are also available, although a permit must be obtained from the Visitor Center.

Apex Park

Apex Park is interesting both from a trail and a historic viewpoint. The Park is however, not very large and will be shared with mountain bikers and hikers. There is ample parking at the lower car lot at Heritage Square, just off US. 40, south of Golden.

An easy going climbing expedition heads up the Mesa Trail

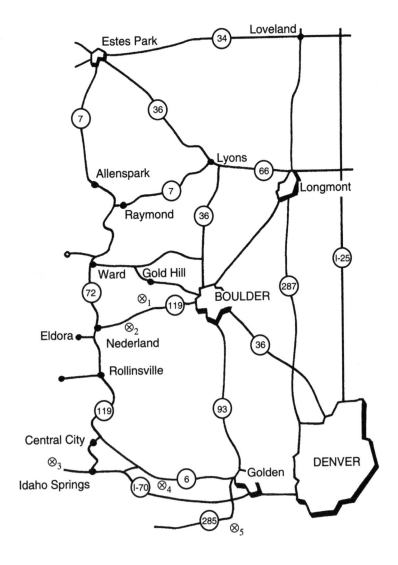

1:       Boulder Falls
2:       Castle Rock
3:       Silver Plume
4:       Clear Creek Canyon
5:       Lovers Leap

Ice Climbing

To the layman, ice climbing must be one of the least comprehensible sports listed in this book. Why go out into the cold, clamber around on a block of ice using seemingly tenuous metal points to adhere to what is essentially a slippery surface, all in the name of sport?

As usual, there are attractions to the sport but they may not be immediately obvious. The Ice Climber's playgrounds can be frozen waterfalls, or rock faces and gullies that collect water, or a mixed terrain of rock and ice. Unlike rock climbing where the rock doesn't change, ice depends upon the weather and therefore can change not only winter to winter, but within days or even hours. This is part of the attraction of the sport - rarely is a route the same each year.

Ice climbing is a skill essential to the mountaineer. Many long routes in the high mountains will involve movement over ice, and therefore the prudent mountaineer will need to learn at least the basic skills. Ice climbing is also a sport in its own right. Some of the best known ice climbs in this area involve a five minute hike from the road - hardly a high mountain experience.

Adherence to the ice does involve the use of specialist ice climbing equipment. Ice axes and crampons are used to actually climb the ice, and ropes, ice screws and pitons are necessary to protect yourself. This equipment, though readily available, does need knowledge to use. And, as this is a risk sport, we strongly urge the beginner to either go with someone experienced, or get instruction from one of the schools operating in the area. Finally, don't forget to wear a helmet at all times, even at the bottom of the route.

Boulder Falls, Boulder Canyon

Located 8 miles up Boulder Canyon, the Boulder Falls are easily identified by having the largest parking lot in the Canyon. A popular, if over-rated tourist attraction, the Falls provide some interesting sport in the winter.

Crossing the road from the lot may be the most dangerous part of the day! The frozen falls are not a great challenge to the experienced yet provide much fun and learning for guide and pupil. Setting up a top-rope can result in a fun few hours, especially if attempted barefooted.

Ice climbing on the icefalls near Castle Rock
Photo: Mark Springett

Castle Rock, Boulder Canyon

Twelve miles up Boulder Canyon lies Castle Rock, home of some excellent summer rock climbs. Just past the crag on the left are twin drainage lines which provide popular ice climbs.

To park, either turn left and descend a short ways on the dirt road that circuits Castle Rock. Park, then cross the frozen creek to the west and follow the creek upstream, ascending gradually. It is a short distance to the two obvious ice falls. The climbs can also be reached more directly from a vehicle pull off a few hundred yards further up the Canyon from Castle Rock.

Icefall #1 is a 90' easy angle slab, whilst #2 is more vertical and about 50' in length. The climbs are often top-roped using natural belays above.

A half mile further up the canyon can be found a larger sheet of ice that also provides good sport.

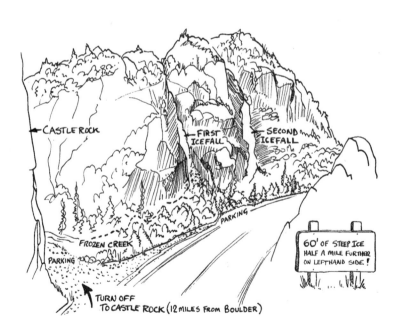

Clear Creek Canyon, Golden

Clear Creek Canyon can be reached by heading south out of Boulder on Hwy. 93 to Golden. Take Hwy. 6 west towards Blackhawk, and enter the canyon.

There are three main areas in the canyon for ice climbing, although there are probably other, less well known, spots. Drive up the canyon for 4½ miles to a point where the creek leaves the left hand side of the road and crosses under a road bridge. Park on the left just before the road bridge. The ice climbing area is back a way. Cross the creek using the bridge and take a path back downstream for a few hundred yards. The ice climb is on the right. You have a choice of either just top-roping the first, often bulging, section, or, to climb the entire climb as a series of steps. The descent is down to the right.

A lesser ice fall is just beyond the bridge. This is a useful alternative if the main area is busy with other enthusiasts.

One other location we know of that is worth looking at is about a mile lower down on the same side of the road.

Ice Screws come in a variety of sizes!

Silver Plume

Located just outside the town of Silver Plume, these falls are a reliable day out. From Boulder take Hwy. 93 south to Golden. Take Clear Creek Canyon Hwy. 6 west to I-70, then follow I-70 west up to Georgetown. 2½ miles beyond is the turning for Silver Plume. Drive off down the ramp and follow the Frontage Road west to the edge of town. Park by a large corrugated iron storage shed.

From the parking area, you can often put your crampons on immediately (not inside your vehicle). The frozen, easy angled, stream bed is tantalizingly close (and just out of sight). Head west parallel to I-70 and the stream will come into view. Follow the stream up, passing under a fallen mine working beam to the beginning of the climb.

Although no more than a ropes length is needed to complete the climb, double ropes are advisable in order to rappel back down. The climb starts easy angled, becomes more stepped until a final steep 20 foot section leads to the top. Beware of the final steep section at the end of the season or when the ice is thin. There is an easy alternative line to the right.

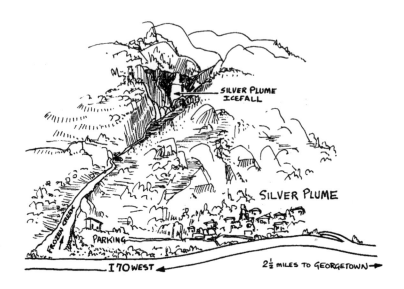

Lovers Leap, Morrison.

Lovers Leap is located in the Canyon west of Morrison on Hwy. 285. From Boulder take Hwy. 93 to Golden, continue south using US 40 to Morrison. At Morrison turn right and then left onto Hwy. 8. Follow this south to Hwy. 285. Turn right towards Conifer. Lovers Leap is the 450' high buttress on the left side of the highway, about 1 mile further on.

To approach the crag, drive past it then double back to the pull-off and parking area just below the crag.

DESCENT: Getting off is a rough and tumble affair down either side. The right hand side is probably the best.

All three routes here will depend upon ice conditions.

1.   Lovers Leap

A serious mixed route. It is recommended to climb it in short (ie. 75') sections making it a five pitch climb. Starts at the middle of the main face. Takes a direct line up corners for the first three pitches. Then leftward to a cave. It is usual to belay above the cave. Final short steep pitch goes through the summit notch, an obvious feature from the parking lot.

2.   Route One

Starts about 100' right of Lovers Leap and climbs a gully and chimney system for a couple of pitches, then traverses right. This brings you to the final crack, which is taken to the top. There is usually more ice higher up the route, with the first section being fairly thin.

3.   Route Two

The approach is via a wide gully, left of the extreme right hand side of the steep buttress. Take a more or less direct line. Joins Route One for the final pitch.

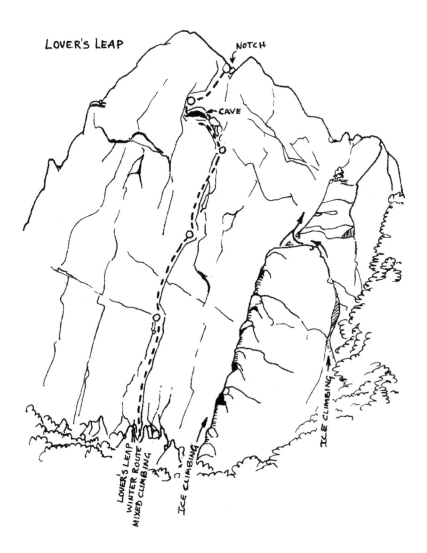

LOVER'S LEAP

NOTCH

CAVE

LOVER'S LEAP
WINTER ROUTE
MIXED CLIMBING

ICE CLIMBING

ICE CLIMBING

Boulder Creek in good style

Inner Tubing

The not-so ancient sport of inner tubing is well established in Boulder. Every Spring young and old alike can be seen idly floating down Boulder Creek on a truck inner tube. To the inexperienced, this appears a simple and relaxing activity. However, there are pit falls for the unwary. Most important is to scout out the section you wish to tube BEFORE you commit yourself to the water. Once on the water you are pretty much at the mercy of the creek.

Boulder Creek is the most popular creek for this sport, with the section from the kayak slalom course down to Broadway being the safest. Areas further upstream are not recommended, and even this lower section could be lethal in very high water. Whilst the most likely injuries from inner tubing will be scrapes and bruises from hitting rocks, be wary of floating down backwards as head injuries could result from hitting a rock from behind. In fact, in our experience, you are more likely to suffer (albeit minor) injuries from this activity than any other in this book.

To reduce the chance of injuries we recommend keeping your backside up to avoid hitting submerged rocks, wear a wetsuit and never tube alone, at night, or under the influence of alcohol or drugs. (In fact, at the risk of preaching, those last four are inappropriate for all the activities listed in this book).

On the lighter side, inner tubing is great fun and there is no better way to cool off when it gets hot.

Finally, stay off the other creeks in the area unless you are absolutely certain that it is safe. Clear Creek for instance may be a fun place to go rafting but can be (and has been) a killer for inner tubers.

Kayaking on the Boulder Creek

Kayaking

Kayaking is a popular sport in this area, despite a lack of really good rivers. The local creeks that are kayakable tend to be fast and shallow, and are therefore quite a bumpy ride. The South Platte however does offer a more mellow experience, as does the lower section of Boulder Creek.

The best season for kayaking is generally May through July, although this varies year to year and is also subject to human intervention. For current flows, check the phone number given at the start of each river description.

Rivers are graded according to difficulty - see the table on the following page - but just as river flows can vary by the hour, so accordingly can the grade. Also, a beginner should be aware that the more difficult rivers are exactly that. Mere 'guts and glory' attitudes will not be much help in violent water if you come out of your boat and no-one can assist you. These rivers can be extremely hostile places to be if you do not know what you are doing.

There are local centers that provide courses and tours on local rivers and they are listed in Reference 3.

The price of plastic kayaks ranges from $600-$800 with the accessories such as a paddle and a life preserver vest running another $300-$400. Used equipment will be less, depending on condition. Plastic kayaks tend to be more suitable for this area because they are very durable, and the rivers locally are going to be bumpy! Fiberglass boats are still available, but will require more maintenance.

In this section we have included descriptions of rivers that are fun to kayak. We are grateful to Eric Bader of the Boulder Outdoor Center for providing these and some of his photographs.

Clear Creek - Georgetown to I-70 and Rt. 6

Length of Trip: 18 miles
Gradient: 50ft/mile start 8,400'
Difficulty: Class III and IV
Flow: Call (303) 831-7135, Division 1, Station 23.
High Water Flows: Mid-May and June, boatable through August. Low water is 200cfs, good water is 350cfs, and high water is above 500 cfs.
Put-In: There are numerous put-ins/take-outs along this section. You can put in just below the Georgetown Lake Dam, but this is not recommended due to the many hazards. The best boating is, by far, from St. Mary's Glacier down to Rt. 6.
Take-Out: Just below the I-70 bridge on Rt. 6, across from Kermits, or the gravel pit on Rt. 6. Shuttle is I-70 to Rt. 6 exit.
Scenery: There are pretty sections on this section, with birds and beaver ponds, but you can hear traffic from I-70, and there are stretches that have been channelized as well as old mining operations beside the river.

Description: If you put in just below the Georgetown Dam, you will find many river hazards, including a road culvert just downstream. The first little bit is class IV with rocks and bushes, so if you run this section, put in where the road crosses the river just below the dam. Continuing downstream you will run into more culverts under I-70, numerous barb-wire fences, at least one low bridge, beaver dams, and several river-wide trees. This section is only suitable for kayaks as canoes and rafts are too high to fit under many of the river hazards, and duckies and inflatable kayaks may also be too high. For kayakers, the ducks, beavers, birds, and sense of adventure somehow makes this run worth doing. Most of the water is class II-III, but the start is class IV, and the obstacles up the rating. Under the Empire Bridge is a class IV rapid, and a full tree blocks the river just downstream.

At the junction of I-70 and Hwy. 40 is another put-in. If you put-in on the West Fork of Clear Creek, you will be able to run a nice class IV rapid just below the confluence with Clear Creek. A little ways down is another put-in at the confluence with the Fall River from St. Mary's Glacier. Park near here, and walk/slide your boat under I-70 into Clear Creek. This section has mostly class IV boating down to Idaho Springs and is a unique run in Colorado as it has been channelized into a pool drop run. This channelization makes this run very runnable in low water. It would be a great section to hang gates for slalom racers to practice racing. The drops along this section come at you fast, and there are blind horizon lines. If you don't know where to run the drop, you should approach the horizon line slowly so you don't charge over the edge into a rock, but if you go slow, you might miss the rock and land in a river wide hole. It is best to bring a probe boater (someone that knows the river well). The first boater can tell the rest of the group behind them where to run the ledges.

At the west end of Idaho Springs, right at the on/off ramp is a put-in or take-out. You can run or put-in below the class IV rapid that lurks just around the corner. Once beyond the class IV rapid at the put-in, the rest of the run is class III in difficulty, with one class IV just above the take-out. Taking a swim on this section is more dangerous than it looks, as, due to its continuous rapids and a lack of eddies, it can be difficult to get out. The last rapid, class IV, is just upstream of the I-70 bridge and the Clear Creek Canyon I-70 exit. This rapid can be portaged on the talus. Take-out just below I-70, on the left. There is a break in the large boulders with a nice eddy.

Idaho Springs to Kermits is about a 5 mile run. Canoes and conventional rafts will have a difficult time due to the continuous nature of this section and the short wave lengths. There are few eddies, if any, to catch once a boat is filled with water.

Grading of Rivers		
I	Easy	Water fast with few or no obstructions
II	Novice	Simple rapids and perhaps rocks
III	Intermediate	More technical, and skill required
IV	Advanced	Powerful water with many hazards
V	Expert	Violent water
VI	Extreme	Right at the limits of the sport

Note: Grades are only an estimate of the difficulty of a particular stretch of water. If in doubt, get out, and check before taking the plunge.

Clear Creek - I-70 to Golden

Length of Trip: 15 miles
Gradient: 105ft/mile average, 160ft/mile max.
Difficulty: Class IV-V at 200-500 CFS, Class V-V+ above 800 CFS
Flow: Call (303) 831-7135, Division 1, Station 22 for current river levels **High Water Flows:** May - July
Put-In: Across from gravel pit, on Hwy. 6, just before the on ramp up to I-70.
Take-Out: Anywhere along Hwy. 6 upstream of Coors. The last take-out is under the Hwy. 6 bridge. Parking is available on Hwy. 6, next to the bridge, or there is a dirt road that is behind the Briarwood Restaurant.
Scenery: This canyon has been mined and follows Hwy. 6.
Description: At the lower flows, this run is a technical run with lots of rocks and eddies. At higher flows, 600+, there are larger waves, holes and faster water. This is a great play river, from eddy hopping to surfing waves, and at high water, 800cfs and up, the velocity of the water is so fast that this run becomes a true hair run. Just past the put-in, there is a rock/tree sieve that may not be runnable, upstream of the first bridge. The next major rapid is upstream of Tunnel 6, and on the outside bend of the tunnel. The river is continuous with class II to IV rapids until you reach Black Rock, at 6.7 road miles. The entrance of Black Rock is marked by a large boulder dividing the river in half. Black Rock rapid is class V, and should be scouted. It got its name from the square black rock next to Hwy. 6. The next major rapid is at 8 road miles, just below Tunnel 2. Scout/take-out just upstream of Hwy. 6 bridge. The Narrows is a long class V rapid with two large holes, one of which which may hold a swimmer. This rapid has been changing from year to year, so always scout it. At 9.8 road miles, the rapid Quiche drops into a couple of large holes and then under a road bridge, class V. You can take-out here or continue to the mouth of the canyon.

The after work run: Put-in just below Quiche. The next 3 miles is continuous class IV+. The first tricky drop is difficult to spot from the road or the river. The drop is called Double Drop, and it involves catching a river left eddie, then paddling right up against an overhanging wall in order to avoid a large river left hole. A great ender spot is at the bottom of this rapid. The next heart throb is the Golf Course, which starts out with a distinct "S" turn, followed by a 6' slide into a ¼ mile of continuous holes and waves. The river eases up just a little as you reach the footbridge above the dam. Right below the footbridge, 12.8 road miles, is the gauging station and a dam. Portaging the dam is highly recommended. Below the dam, the river is class III, with branches and a diversion dam on river left, run right, until you reach Hwy. 93.

Just upstream of the Hwy. 93 bridge is a great play hole. The hole is well-developed at almost all river levels, and although it looks scary, it's a great deal of fun. River right of the hole is private property. It is best to scout this river by vehicle before running.

Eric Bader away from the office
Photo: Mike Bader

Boulder Creek - Boulder Canyon Tunnel to Slalom Course

Length of Trip: 3 miles
Gradient: 145ft/mile
Difficulty: Class IV+ at 200-500 CFS
Flow: Call (303) 831-7135, Division 1, Station 9 for current river levels, in Boulder Canyon. Water releases on the creek are controlled by computers, so river flows will change dramatically.
High Water Flows: May-June
Put-In: Drive up the canyon 4.6 miles from Arapahoe, then turn left on a dirt road at mile marker 38 just before the tunnel. Put in at the gauging station. The gauge should read about 2.0 or better for the creek to be runable.
Take-Out: At, or just upstream, of Eben G. Fine Park, the west side of Boulder, at the mouth of Boulder Canyon where Arapahoe and Canyon meet, or you can continue through town.
Scenery: The City of Boulder has built a bike and pedestrian path along the creek and the road follows the river.
Description: At the lower flows, this run is a technical run with lots of rocks and eddies. At higher flows, 300+, there are waves, holes and fast water. The first time you make this run, consider the run an easy class V, (if there is such a thing as an easy class V) as the speed of the water in the last rapid will make the run seem harder than it is. The second time you make the run, you will understand that the water is fast, but the rapids are straightforward. Watch out for dead fall, branches, and the culvert at the Red Lion. Run the left culvert of the Red Lion bridge, if it is clear of debris. At high water, scout this drop before you run, as eddies are lacking. The most difficult rapid is a ½ mile upstream from the intersection of Arapahoe and Canyon. The river carves a left turn with large holes, waves and rocks. The continuousness makes it difficult to stop. Scout! High water runs are rare on Boulder Creek, but if the water is high, watch out for low water pipes. This run has fun little micro eddies, waves and a few holes to play. It makes a great after-work run, especially since there is a better chance of water releases on weekday evenings.

Boulder Creek - Slalom Course through Boulder

Length of Trip: Up to 5 miles
Gradient: 25ft/mile to 130ft/mile max
Difficulty: Class II-III at 200-500 CFS.
Flow: Call (303) 831-7135, Division 1, Station 9 for current river levels, in Boulder Canyon or Division 1, Station 8 for flows east of town at 75th. Please note that a great deal of water diversion occurs along the creek, so the run through town may not have the water reported by the flow phone. Water releases on the creek are controlled by computers, so river flows can change dramatically, even while you are on the river.
High Water Flows: May-July
Put-In: At or just upstream of Eben G. Fine Park, at the mouth of Boulder Canyon where Arapahoe and Canyon meet.
Take-Out: Anywhere along the Boulder Creek corridor that is city owned. Many boaters use the take-out near Jose Muldoons restaurant on the corner of Arapahoe and 38th. From the river, the take-out is on river left, just under the Arapahoe bridge. Additional common take-outs are at the Valmont bridge and at the 75th bridge. Between Valmont and 75th is a dam without a boat chute, please portage. Beyond 75th is private property where people dislike boaters so please take-out at 75th.
Scenery: The City of Boulder has built a linear park through town along the creek. There is a pedestrian path and a bike path that a great number of people use. The stream bed has also been altered by the City of Boulder, so the entire run is man-made.
Description: At the lower flows, this run is a technical run with lots of rocks and eddies. At higher flows, 400+, there are waves, small nasty man-made holes and faster water. As you head east through town, the river gets easier, with less rocks and waves. When the creek goes under Arapahoe for the second time, the river turns into a class I-II run. This run is great for accomplished novices and up, but please keep in mind that the creek is not very deep, with fast water, which will abuse beginners should they flip. Please start beginner boaters on easier or deeper water. The creek lacks good shore eddies for novices, especially for rescues. Boaters can scout the entire run from the bikepath before running. At the mouth of the canyon, under Arapahoe at its junction with Canyon, there is a slalom course which can be boated any time the

creek is free of ice. The stream bed has been altered to allow boating in extremely low flows. This section is mostly class II with one class III in the middle and a class III under the pedestrian bridge just below the race course. The slalom course is open to all and has some fun, sticky hole playing. The less aggressive paddlers can put-in at the bottom of Eben G. Fine Park. The dams in town now have boat chutes around them with signs marking which side of the river to run. Between Foothills Parkway and 55th Street is an area known as Cottonwood Farm. This is owned by the city and access is restricted to preserve the flora and fauna. Please stay on the creek through this area.

Mike Bader doing an 'ender' for the camera
Photo: Eric Bader

South Platte - Brighton City Park to Ft. Lupton

Length of Trip: 7 miles
Gradient: 20 ft/mile
Difficulty: Class I-I+ at 200+ CFS with one portage river right
Flow: Call (303) 831-7135, Division 1, Station 48 for current river levels at-the take out.
High Water Flows: May - July, boatable year-round.
Put-In: North of Denver, take Rt. 7 east from I-25 for 8.4 miles, to Veterans Park on the north side.
Take-Out: From the put-in, go east on Rt. 7 for 0.4 miles, north on Hwy 85 for 6.2 miles to 52nd West (Dacona) exit. Go west on 52nd for 0.1 miles to the bridge over the river. This is the take-out.
Scenery: There are many birds, cottonwood trees, and other wildlife. Hwy. 85 is not very far from the river, so you can hear vehicles at times, and manmade debris can be found in and along the river. The views of the Rockies and the wildlife help offset the debris and the highway to make this an enjoyable run.
Description: This run is a great first time river experience for all kinds of river boats and novice river runners. The river is mostly flat with some current. At higher flows, the current will pick up speed, but the river difficulty will not change until the river is over its banks in flood. This run does have its river hazards to be aware of. There are many strainers (giant cotton wood trees in the river), bridge abutments, fences along the shore and into the water, cement blocks on the banks and into the water, pieces of steel, all with debris piled up on them, and one dam in the middle of the run. The dam is relatively easy to spot. On river left is a cement wall and in the middle of the river is a large rock monolith. The dam goes between these items. Portage river right. This dam has been run, but the difficulty will vary with water levels, and debris caught in the dam. Always scout this drop as the debris will change any runnable spot from day to day. Dams are much more dangerous than their technical difficulty, so please portage.

Even with all these hazards, this run is still a good run for beginners, you just need to be a little careful. The water is warm compared to other rivers in Colorado. There are eddies to catch, small waves to surf, and a meandering channel to find in the river bed. There are also sand beaches to enjoy and camping spots among the cottonwoods. Depending on the time of year, you can expect to see: Great Blue Herons, Whooping Cranes, King Fishers, Turtles up to 18" across, Ducks, Muskrats, and much more.
All in all, a great river for, kayaks, canoes, rafts, duckies, sea kayaks, and most any other boat that can be run down rivers.

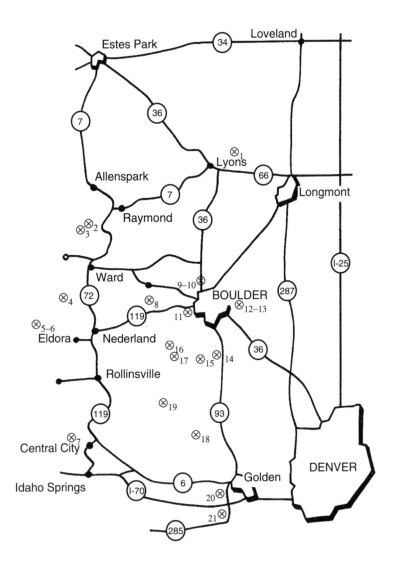

1:	Rabbit Mountain	8:	Switzerland Trail
2:	Bunce School Road	9:	Foothills Trail
3:	Peaceful Valley Loop	10:	Foothills & Cottonwood
4:	Sourdough Trail	11:	Boulder Creek
5:	Fourth of July	12:	East Boulder
6:	Eldora to Caribou	13:	South Boulder
7:	Cemetery Loop	14:	Community Ditch

15:	Rattlesnake Gulch
16:	Meyers Homestead
17:	Walker Ranch Loop
18:	White Ranch
19:	Deer Creek
20:	Apex Park
21:	Matthews Winters Park

Mountain Biking

A casual observer might be excused for thinking that the Holy Grail of mountain biking in the Boulder area is the Boulder Creek Trail, judging by the hordes that zoom up and down it. Whilst it is probably true that some of these $1,000 machines rarely see a mountain, Boulder certainly has some demanding rides nearby. In fact there are trails for all in the area, with, as a general rule, more technical rides up in the mountains and down near Golden, and more mellow rides within the immediate vicinity of the town.

During the early years of the sport, some of the local open space areas suffered badly from undisciplined riding which led ultimately to bikes being banned from many areas. In order that this trend does not continue, particularly with the ever increasing pressure on the few remaining open areas, it is important to ride only on marked trails and not to make new trails or take shortcuts.

Some of the mountain trails will be blocked by snow drifts through to June, so it's worth checking you can get through before arranging to be dropped off for something like the Sourdough Trail. For help on this, contact one of the biking shops in town to see if they know whether your intended route is open. We have listed some of the towns numerous biking stores in Reference 2.

You are advised to carry with you at all times, but most importantly when in the outlying regions, a spares kit consisting of: spare inner tube, puncture repair kit, pump and basic tool set. Plenty of drinking water is always advisable, and a helmet should be standard equipment.

Rabbit Mountain

Distance: 3½ miles of trails
Difficulty: Easy
Terrain: Dirt track
Time Required: Half day
Start elevation: 5,400'   **Elevation gain:** 660'

Not wildly exciting biking, but a good trip nonetheless. It does offer a different perspective on the plains and the Foothills. Also a good viewpoint for Longs Peak (14,255').

Take Hwy. 36 from Boulder north to Lyons. At the junction with Hwy. 66, turn right and then left soon after (at the orange water tank) on 53rd which leads onto N. 55th. Street. The trailhead is a short distance further north, about 4 miles from Hwy. 66.

Trail heads east and up onto a saddle where a dirt track leads off to the left. This rather rocky trail leads to the Little Thompson Overlook. Just after the junction for the Little Thompson Overlook, a road branches off to the right. Along here - about a 1/2 mile - there is a track leading off to the right. This - the Eagle Wind Trail - follows the ridge for a short distance.

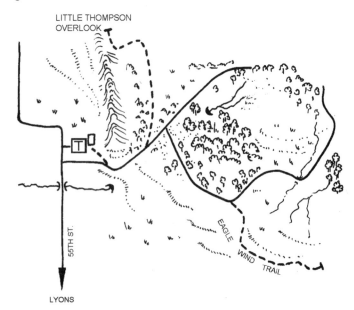

Bunce School Road

Distance: 6 miles one way
Difficulty: Moderate
Terrain: Dirt road
Time Required: Half day
Start elevation: 8,630' **Elevation gain:** 250'

Trail starts at the Peaceful Valley Campground which is on CR. 92 just off Hwy. 72 at Peaceful Valley, 6 miles north of Ward.

An initial steep uphill section can be a bit of a struggle, but from then on it's a gentle descent towards Allenspark. At Hwy. 72 you can turn around and return, or make a loop by taking Hwy. 7 south to the junction with Hwy. 72, which is then followed back to Peaceful Valley.

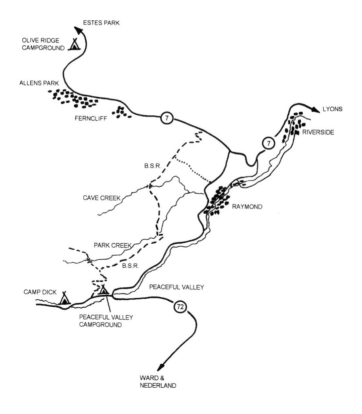

Peaceful Valley Loop

Distance: 8½ miles round trip
Difficulty: Difficult & strenuous
Terrain: Dirt track
Time Required: Full day
Start elevation: 8,638' **Elevation gain:** 1,182'

An interesting day out, and although the first section is very rocky and technical, the trail does improve. There may be snow drifts blocking sections of the trail through to June.

Trail starts at Camp Dick which is on CR. 92 just off Hwy. 72 at Peaceful Valley, 6 miles north of Ward.

The trail heads west following the Middle St. Vrain Road for about 3.5 miles to an obvious signed junction. Take a left here - Road #507 - and head uphill along a narrower trail. This joins Road #961 after ½ mile. The trail then heads back east, bordering Beaver Reservoir to join the Sourdough Trail. Take a left and ride downhill back to the trailhead.

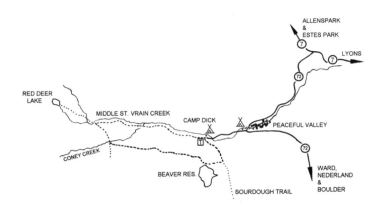

Sourdough Trail

Distance: 11 miles one way
Difficulty: Difficult
Terrain: Narrow path with rocks and tree roots
Time Required: Full day
Start elevation: 9,200' **Elevation gain:** 1,040'

The ever popular Sourdough Trail is a scenic ride, mainly through trees with occasional views, and offers interesting riding. There may be snow drifts blocking sections of the trail through to June.

Trail starts on CR. 116 which is off Hwy. 72, 7 miles north of Nederland towards Ward. CR. 116 is sign posted for the University of Colorado Mountain Research Station. There is limited parking at the trail head.

The Sourdough heads north from the trailhead (this is also a Cross-Country Ski trail so it is blazed with blue diamonds) through the trees. After 6 miles cross the Brainard Lake Road and continue up to the Beaver Reservoir Road. From here, you can turn around and return, or continue down into Peaceful Valley if you left a second car at Camp Dick.

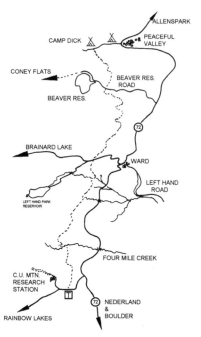

Fourth of July

Distance: 5 miles one way
Difficulty: Moderate
Terrain: Jeep trail
Time Required: Half day
Start elevation: 9,010' **Elevation gain:** 1,070'

The Fourth of July Campground is also known as the Buckingham Campground.

From Nederland, drive south on Hwy. 72 for a short distance before taking a right towards Eldora. Drive through Eldora and just after the road turns to a jeep trail a junction is reached. There is parking here or just before the junction. Take care not to block the road.

The Fourth of July Trail follows the right fork from the junction as it goes up a gentle, uphill jeep track to the Fourth of July Campground. The views from here are spectacular and well worth the trip. The left fork at the trailhead goes to the town site of Hessie and this makes a pleasant out-and-back detour.

Marmot

Eldora to Caribou

Distance: 6 miles one way, 17 round trip via Nederland
Difficulty: Difficult
Terrain: Jeep trail
Time Required: Full day
Start elevation: 8,750' **Elevation gain:** 1,490'

Attractions include the ghost town of Caribou and evidence of the area's mining past.

From Nederland, drive south on Hwy. 72 for a short distance before taking a right towards Eldora. The trail starts from Washington Street on the west side of town - just off Huron Street. Parking is limited.

Follow the jeep trail as it heads initially east, climbing the side of Eldorado Mountain and then heads back northwest. After about 4 miles the gradient eases as you arrive at Caribou Flats. Continue north then down to the old silver mining town site of Caribou. This is now a quiet meadow, but was once a booming town of 3,000 people. From Caribou, turn around and return, or follow the Caribou road back east into Nederland. Take Hwy. 72 south until the turn for Eldora, then back along CR. 130 to Eldora.

Central City

Central City is quite an experience for those unused to the power that gambling can exert. The whole town seems to be geared now towards gambling, and visitors not intending to gamble can feel almost unwelcome. Be aware that parking can be expensive unless you also visit the saloons to get a 'Refund'. Extortion appears to be alive and well here.

In spite of this, the town has a charm of its own and the Cemetery Loop Trail gives an interesting insight into a bygone era.

Warning: You are advised to keep well clear of the old mine workings. Most are in a very unstable condition and represent a considerable hazard to the adventurous (foolhardy).

Cemetery Loop

Distance: 8½ miles round trip
Difficulty: Moderate
Terrain: Jeep track
Time Required: Half day
Start elevation: 8,965' **Elevation gain:** 565'

Among its many attractions, this area boasts interesting old mine workings and cemeteries. The aspen groves, particularly in the fall, also make it worthwhile.

Drive through Central City heading straight west as the road - Lawrence Street - climbs out of town. At the top, park at one of several parking areas around the cemeteries here. The Boodle Mill is across the street.

Cycle back down Lawrence Street into town, and at the stop sign take a right, past the shops and a small information booth on the left. Then take the right fork up towards the obvious hillside parking lots. This street heads to Nevadaville. Grunt your way up to the almost deserted Nevadaville. Continue through the town and on up. After reaching the small saddle, head down to the four way intersection and take a left. The trail descends passing Bald Mountain Cemetery on the right and continues on, taking always the right fork at intersections until you arrive on FS Road 175. It is not unusual to get lost here - see the detail map opposite. Slightly further on, at an intersection popular for parking jeeps, take the right fork - marked 7010 - and head down into a valley. The trail continues down, taking a right fork followed by a right junction to arrive back at the cemeteries where you parked.

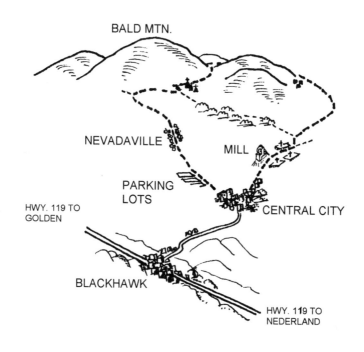

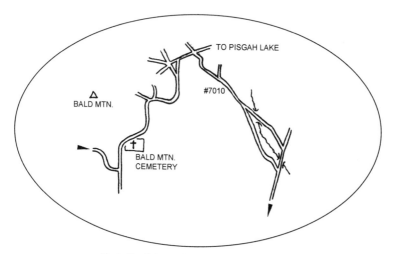

Detail of the mid section of the trail

Switzerland Trail

Distance: 9-13 miles one way, 22 miles into Boulder
Difficulty: Easy
Terrain: Jeep Trail
Time Required: Half day
Start elevation: 8,470' **Elevation gain:** 130'

The Switzerland Trail follows an old railroad route through scenic country and is popular with beginners and families. It gently descends to the town of Sunset then rises up to meet the Gold Hill Road.

Take Boulder Canyon west towards Nederland. About 4 miles out of town, take the Sugar Loaf Road right. Follow for 10 miles until junction with Sugar Loaf Mountain Road goes off to the right. Follow this for 1 mile to the trailhead.

The trail is pretty straight forward and getting lost is not usual. From the junction at the Gold Hill Road, you have three options. 1) to return the way you came; 2) to continue on the trail to end on the Sawmill Road (rather pointless); and 3) turn right and head to Gold Hill. Rich gold deposits were found locally in the spring of 1859. Gold Hill has a old world feel about it, and the Inn is renowned for good food and beer. From Gold Hill, take the long downhill to Boulder via Sunshine Canyon. Retrieving the car from the start will require either a second car or hitching back up.

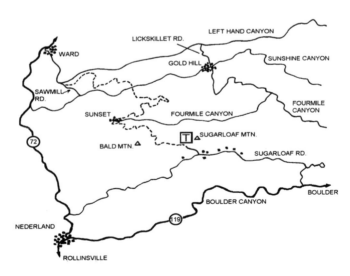

Foothills Trail

Distance: 5 miles one way
Difficulty: Moderate
Terrain: Dirt trail
Time Required: Half day

Attractions include Wonderland Lake, and foothills flora and fauna.

The trail starts at Wonderland Lake, which is located north on Broadway out of town. Park at the Foothills Nature Center, located at 4201 N. Broadway, opposite Sumac Avenue.

Take the trail west past Wonderland Lake and then head north on an 'improved' trail. Cross Lee Hill Road and follow the trail as it contours the hillside. A steep descent leads back down and under Hwy. 36 by way of an underpass, to the Foothills Trailhead. Take a left at the junction here and follows the dirt road for a short distance before crossing a mesa and then a short steep descent to another dirt road. Follow this east to the Boulder Reservoir, skirting a small unnamed reservoir en route. At the trailhead overlooking Boulder Reservoir turn around and return.

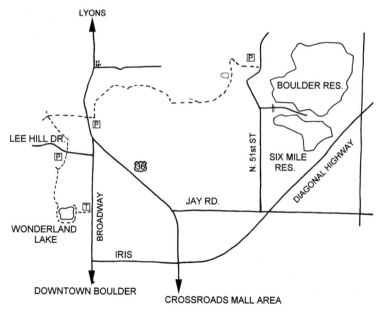

Foothills & Cottonwood Loop

Distance: 15 miles round trip
Difficulty: Moderate
Terrain: Dirt trail, road and concrete paths
Time Required: Half day

FOOTHILLS & COTTONWOOD LOOP

HEAD OUT OF TOWN, WEST ON PEARL

TAKE 4th STREET NORTH TO KALMIA

CONTINUE EAST AND ACROSS LINDEN

FOLLOW BIKE PATH ON LEFT

SKIRT WONDERLAND LAKE TO JOIN FOOTHILLS TRAIL

FOLLOW FOOTHILLS TRAIL TO BOULDER RESERVOIR
        (SEE PREVIOUS DESCRIPTION)

AT THE RESERVOIR TRAILHEAD, GO SOUTH ON
        51st STREET TO JAY ROAD

EAST ON JAY, ACROSS THE DIAGONAL HIGHWAY

COTTONWOOD STARTS JUST PAST THE DIAGONAL

FOLLOW COTTONWOOD SOUTH TO INDEPENDENCE

TAKE CONCRETE PATH PAST HAYDEN LAKE
        AND THROUGH HOUSING DEVELOPMENT

JOIN VALMONT ROAD

FOLLOW VALMONT, WEST ON FOOTHILLS PARKWAY,
        THEN SOUTH ON EAST SIDE OF HIGHWAY
        TO THE BOULDER CREEK PATH

AT BOULDER CREEK PATH, FOLLOW IT BACK
        INTO TOWN

Boulder Creek Trail

Distance:	7 miles one way
Difficulty:	Easy
Terrain:	Concrete path
Time Required:	Not a lot

Includes a fish observatory, prairie dog homes, sculptures, wildlife and the usual eclectic mix of Boulder inhabitants!

The trail technically starts at the east side of 55th Street, near the junction with Valmont, and ends at the junction of Canyon Boulevard and Four Mile Canyon. However, there are numerous access points along its length, allowing for a more flexible approach.

The Boulder Creek Trail winds its way through the center of Boulder and up into the foothills, offering a wide range of experiences along the way! The trail can get very crowded, particularly at weekends and in the midsection near the center of town. Be conscious of all other path users and observe the speed limits. The path is patrolled and radar traps are not uncommon. For trail drawing see page 103.

IMBA (International Mountain Bicycling Association) Rules of the Trail

Ride only on open trails. Avoid riding on private land without asking permission. Respect trail closures.

Leave no trace. Ride in a manner that will leave no trace of your having passed. Erosion of trails is increased when the soil is wet after rain or snow melt. Do not cut corners or create new trails.

Control your bicycle. Always be alert to other trail users and ride at a safe speed.

Always yield the trail. When approaching other trail users from behind, make your presence known - try a friendly greeting, or use a bell.

Never spook animals. If you meet a horse and rider, it is usually safer to dismount and let them pass. In any event, respect the fact that horses can be dangerous if startled. Disturbing wild animals is an offense, as well as dangerous.

Plan ahead. Know your equipment and ability, and choose your trail accordingly.

East Boulder Trail

Distance: 7 miles one way
Difficulty: Easy
Terrain: Dirt road & track
Time Required: Not a lot

     A popular trail for all users, it is mainly level until the final rise up to the Mesa. During the summer months, myriads of flying insects can provide sustenance unless you keep your mouth shut.

     The trail starts at the Teller Farm Trailhead located just off Arapahoe Avenue, 1 mile east of 75th Street.

     The trail trends north on a dirt road until reaching Valmont Drive. At Valmont the trail heads west briefly, crosses the road, then continues north again. Another lake is passed - look out for a heron - and then after crossing Boulder Creek, the trail starts to climb up onto the Mesa. Some way further on it meets the Gunbarrel Farm Trail. You can either turn left or right on this trail, or more logically, turn around and head back.

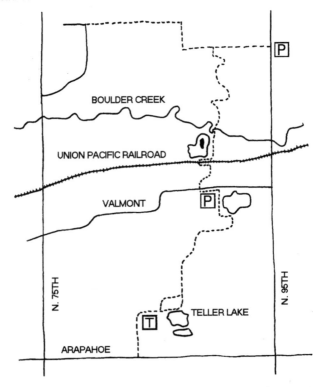

South Boulder Trail

Distance: 3 miles one way
Difficulty: Easy
Terrain: Dirt trail
Time Required: Not a lot

Interesting wetland habitat which boasts a wide variety of birds. There is also a self-guided Nature Trail for the first section.

Starts at the Bobolink Trailhead on Baseline Road just west of Cherryvale Road.

This largely level trail heads south along the creek, to a slight detour for an underpass below South Boulder Road. Head back west to rejoin the trail. The trail ends abruptly at a small lake outside Marshall. The midsection of the trail, by the South Boulder Road, can become very muddy during the Spring.

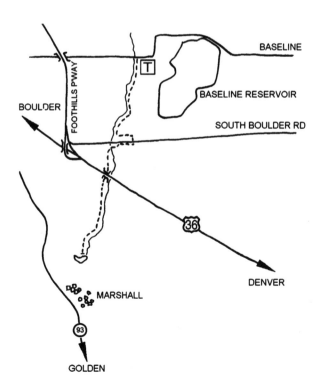

Community Ditch Trail

Distance: 5 miles one way
Difficulty: Easy
Terrain: Dirt trail
Time Required: Not a lot

This trail starts at the Doudy Draw trailhead on the south side of Hwy. 170, 1.5 miles west of Hwy. 93.

From the trailhead, follow the trail south to the picnic area and restrooms. From here head east on the Community Ditch trail which is followed until the junction with Hwy. 93. Cross Hwy. 93 and continue along the trail almost to Marshall Reservoir. The trail avoids the Reservoir - no public access - and then zig-zags down to the Marshall Mesa Trailhead.

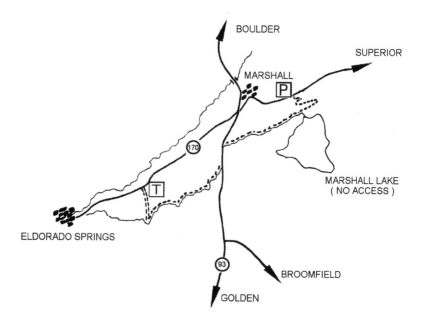

Rattlesnake Gulch

Distance: 2 miles one way
Difficulty: Difficult and strenuous
Terrain: Dirt trail
Time Required: Half day
Start elevation: 5,680' **Elevation gain:** 1,500'

Rattlesnake Gulch is quite an interesting ride for those keen on technical riding, otherwise there are better quality rides in the Boulder area.

This trail is inside the Eldorado Canyon State Park. Take Hwy. 93 south out of Boulder, and after about 5 miles, turn right at the junction for Eldorado Springs (Hwy. 170). Drive through Eldorado Springs and enter the park (Fee required). The nearest parking is about a ½ mile further on.

The trail follows the Fowler Trail initially, then forks right. The next short section is quite technical, but the trail then becomes more of a standard grunt as it winds its way up the hillside. At about the halfway point the ruins of the old Crags Hotel are reached. The trail becomes narrower from here on as it climbs up to finish at the railway line. Trains pass by here regularly on their way across the Rockies.

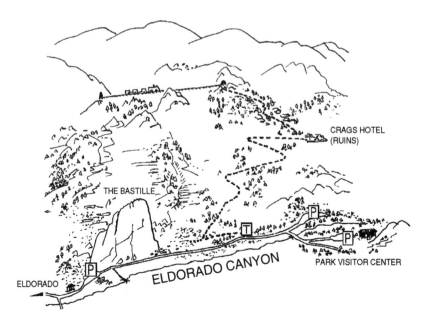

Meyers Homestead Trail

Distance: 2½ miles one way
Difficulty: Easy
Terrain: Dirt trail
Time Required: Not a lot
Start elevation: 7,440'   **Elevation gain:** 455'

The Meyers Homestead Trail is a pleasant ride through trees and meadows past an old homestead site. Great views towards the mountains from the overlook at the trail end.

Meyers Homestead is on the Walker Ranch. From Boulder, take Baseline up over Flagstaff and on past Kossler Lake. Walker Ranch is about 9 miles out of town. Starts at the trailhead and group picnic area on the right, just before the left turn to the Walker Ranch Historic Site.

This is a gentle ride on a wide trail through meadows and ends at a scenic overlook.

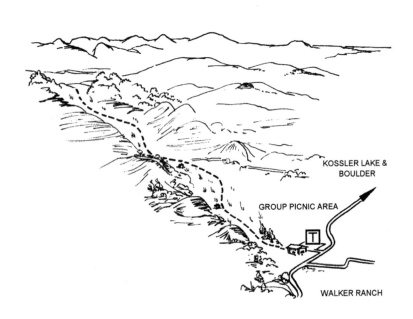

Walker Ranch Loop Trail

Distance: 8 miles round trip
Difficulty: Difficult
Terrain: Narrow trails , rocks and roots
Time Required: Half day
Start elevation: 6,700' **Elevation gain:** 400'

Technically interesting. This area has a remote feeling and great views. Probably the best mountain bike trail in the Boulder area.

Trail starts at the South Boulder Creek Trailhead. From Boulder, take Baseline up over Flagstaff and on past Kossler Lake. Walker Ranch is about 9 miles out of town. Just past the group picnic area on the right and where the road does a sharp right, a stony road goes off and down to the left. Follow this for a short distance to the trailhead.

From the trailhead, start by descending the South Boulder Creek Trail to the creek. Take the left after crossing the creek, then ascend steeply up to join the Gross Reservoir Road which leads to the Crescent Meadows parking lot. From here, cross the meadows on the Crescent Meadows Trail, and follow this down as it becomes increasingly steep and technical. Eventually it becomes so steep that riding becomes impossible. Carry your bike for the final short section down to the creek. Cross the creek using the footbridge then hang a left on the Eldorado Canyon Trail. This is followed more gently up to the trailhead on Bison Road. Breeze back along Bison, then Pika to emerge on the Flagstaff Road just north of the Walker Ranch turning.

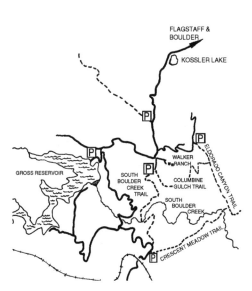

White Ranch

Directions: Take Broadway south out of Boulder and continue on Hwy. 93 towards Golden. The ranch is sign posted off to the right - W. 56th, 17 miles out of Boulder. The trail head is 1½ miles further on. The Ranch is administered by Jefferson County Open Space. Telephone: (303) 271-5925.

Horses and their riders are often encountered at White Ranch. Always stop and let the horse and rider come past. Remember, the ranch is multi-use and mutual respect will help it stay that way, to everyone's advantage.

The interconnecting nature of the trails at the ranch makes it possible to choose your own routes according to fitness, weather and inclination. A popular route, however, is the circular one around the rim of the ranch.

White Ranch Loop Trail

Distance: 14 miles round trip
Difficulty: Difficult & strenuous
Terrain: Narrow Trail
Time Required: Half day
Start elevation: 6,150' **Elevation gain:** 1,721'

This trail can be started from the east side trailhead , or from the trailhead on the west side of the ranch. The description below is for the east side start.

Take the trail from the trailhead and climb effortlessly up Belcher Hill Trail to where it meets the Mustang Trail. Follow Mustang more gently to the trailhead on west side of the ranch. Cross the road and continue on the Belcher Hill Trail for a short stretch to join the Rawhide Trail again. Follow this around the northern part of the ranch. Drinking water can be obtained at the Sourdough Springs Campsite. Where the Rawhide Trail joins the Longhorn Trail, follow the Longhorn Trail south to rejoin the Belcher Hill Trail. This section is the most technical.

While it sounds a complicated route, you are unlikely to go far wrong if you take a left at all trail junctions (for a clockwise direction).

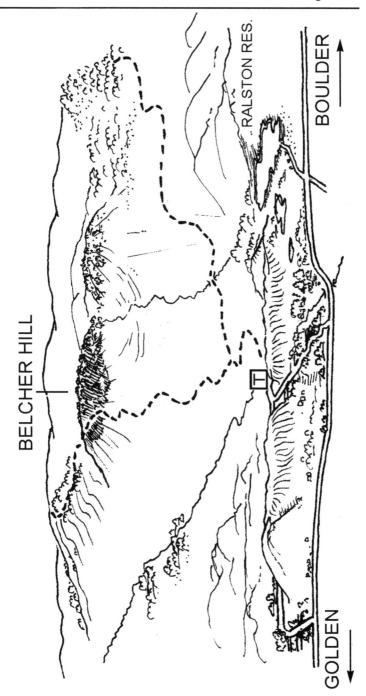

Golden Gate Canyon State Park

For more information on the Golden Gate Canyon State Park, see the entry for the Frazer Meadow Loop Trail in the hiking section.

Golden Gate Canyon State Park allows mountain biking in the section within Jefferson County. They are not allowed within the Gilpin County section of the park.

Deer Creek Loop Trail

Distance: 8 miles round trip
Difficulty: Difficult
Terrain: Narrow dirt trail
Time Required: Half day
Start elevation: 7,760' **Elevation gain:** 1,040'

The Golden Gate Canyon State Park can be accessed most easily from Boulder by driving to Nederland, then following Hwy. 72 south. When Hwy. 72 breaks east, continue south on Hwy.119 towards Central City. A turning is reached on the left for the park about 3 miles south of Rollinsville. Take this as it enters the north-west section of the park. Hang a right at the park pay station, and follow this road down into the park. At the Kriley Pond junction, turn left towards the Visitor Center. Turn left at the Visitor Center and follow the Ralston Creek for about 3 miles to a turning to the left for the Nott Creek Trailhead.

From the trailhead, head up the hillside following the Mountain Lion Trail. After a short steep section, it levels out through meadows then descends down to the Deer Creek. Continue on the Mountain Lion Trail as it follows the creek uphill. This section can be rather trying as large boulders impede progress in places. After about a mile or so, the trail leaves the creek and heads steeply uphill zigzagging through the trees to reach a ridge. The descent from the ridge more than makes up for the tedious creek section. You pass the cabins and ponds at the idyllic Forgotten Valley before heading uphill again to join the Eagle Trail. Follow this as it winds its way along the hillside above the road to a short steep downhill section brings you back to the trailhead.

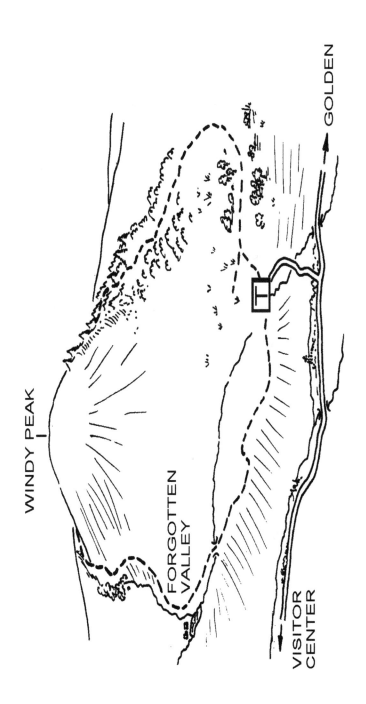

Apex Park

Distance: 5 mile round trip, 6½ miles with extra loop
Difficulty: Difficult
Terrain: Narrow dirt trail
Time Required: Half day
Start elevation: 6,180'   **Elevation gain:** 1,030'

Park at lower car lot at Heritage Square, just off US. 40, south of Golden.

Follow the Apex Trail uphill, over the bridge and into the park. The trail follows the stream for about ¾ mile, past the start of the Sledge Trail to where the Sluicebox Trail begins on the right. Take Sluicebox as it zig-zags up the hillside. The gradient is not too painful. Cross Pick Trail and continue uphill for not much further. There then follows a pleasant descent through the trees along Grubstake as it then curls around, back into the open again before joining Sledge on a ridge. From here you can follow Sledge down to where it joins the Apex Trail at the stream and then back to the trailhead. Or, a short loop can be done by taking Pick back uphill, then following Grubstake again as it goes over the top of the hill to where you can pick up Bonanza to rejoin Grubstake.

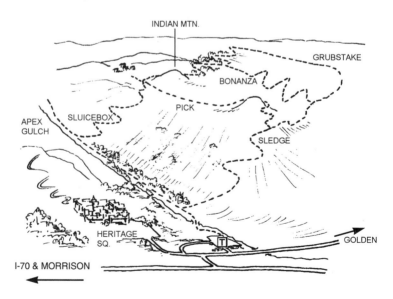

Mountain biking near Eldora
Photo: Anne Krause

Matthews Winters Park

Distance: 5 miles round trip
Difficulty: Difficult
Terrain: Narrow dirt trail
Time Required: Half day
Start elevation: 6,240'   **Elevation gain:** 570'

A technically interesting ride, considered by some to be the best in the area. There is also a Dinosaur self-guided trail part way round which is worth a butcher's hook*.

Park at the parking lot off Hwy. 26, just south of the junction of I-70 & US. 40, outside of Golden.

This can be ridden in either direction, but clockwise is probably better. From the lot, cross over US 40 and take the trail as it angles up to the Dakota Ridge. Once on the ridge, follow it pleasurably along to the road cutting. The cutting marks the middle of the Dinosaur Trail. The trail continues the other side of the road and briefly regains the ridge before hurtling down to US 40 again. It crosses this and follows the road opposite towards Red Rocks for a short distance before breaking right and uphill. Cross another small road and head into an area with characteristic red rock formations. The trail splits just up here. For those with the lung capacity, the higher trail, Morrison Slide, gives good sport, otherwise take the lower trail of Red Rocks. They rejoin later and complete the trail by crossing the meadows area that was once the site of Mt. Vernon Town.

* *Butcher's Hook: East End of London rhyming slang for 'have a look'.*

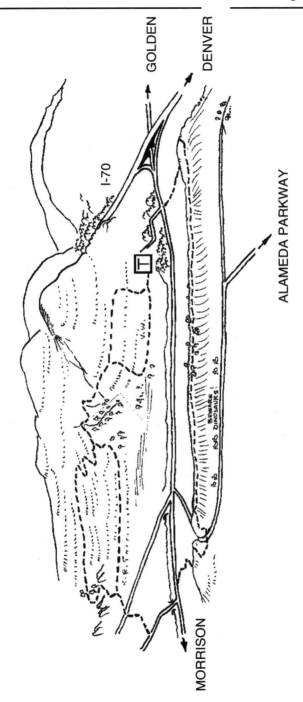

Onward and Upward!

Mountaineering

Mountaineering is the skill of combining rock climbing, snow and ice techniques, along with hiking and general outdoor knowledge. Putting all these elements together can allow you to climb mountains by possibly a tougher than average route.

This is one of the more serious sections of the book. There are no half-day trips. Often it is best to leave at first light (sometimes even before sunrise) in order to achieve your objective. You may be able to see some of the routes listed here from the parking lot at King Soopers on 30th Street - but be warned, it's a different world up around 12,000 feet!

Dealing with objective dangers becomes part of the adventure. Knowing when to retreat is a quintessential trait of a good mountaineer. Remember, the mountains will always be there! As you are in the mountains, you are subject to the particular climactic and natural conditions that can turn a sunny day into a howling blizzard. These greater objective dangers include, amongst others, avalanche, lightning strikes, rock fall, hypothermia and frostbite. For these reasons, the climbs noted here are a more serious undertaking than most of the climbs in the rock climbing section. We urge, therefore, that considerable caution be exercised before setting out on the following climbs. Get instruction, or go with someone with experience, rather than learn the hard way.

A good way to get into the sport is to join the Colorado Mountaineering Club - they have a branch based at Chautauqua Park in Boulder. They run courses in most of the major aspects of getting around the mountains safely.

Navajo Peak - via the Navajo Snowfield

Steep snow & rock climbing
All day. Ice axe, crampons, rope and helmet required
A serious undertaking

One of the great mixed climbs of the Indian Peaks. As the Navajo Snowfield remains all year around, this makes a great summer route.

From Nederland drive north on Hwy. 72 to Ward. Just after the Ward turning, take the left to Brainard Lake. Follow this road around Brainard Lake to the Long Lake Trailhead.

From the trailhead, hike the Pawnee Pass Trail along the right hand side of Long Lake, and continue on past Lake Isabelle on its northern shore. The Pawnee Pass Trail turns right before the lake. From Lake Isabelle, the day takes on a more remote feeling as you pass under the imposing east face of Mt. Shoshoni on the right. The snowfield, visible for much of the walk, finally appears within reach. You should be able to make out whether anyone has skied it recently! Soon you will see the waterfall fed by the Isabelle Glacier on your right. In this upper area on the west side of Shoshoni lie the Shoshoni couloirs. Ahead lies the small unnamed lake, before the final short steep approach to the bottom of the snowfield. The snowfield is approximately 1,000 feet in length.

Either ascend the snowfield diagonally from bottom right up to the col containing an 80' pinnacle called, rather rudely, Dicker's Peck, or climb the steeper left hand side direct to the col.

On gaining the col, pleasant and easy climbing of several rope pitches at around the 5.2 grade lead to the summit of Navajo Peak. The only major obstacle is a steep 12' high crack with bountiful holds. After this, it's all over except to savor the views (bring a good map and compass to help identify distant peaks and in case of bad weather).

It may be necessary to rappel to the north-west and traverse the south side of the summit pyramid eastward to join the Niwot Ridge. Keep a sharp eye out to the left (north) for the descent gully called Airplane Gully (so called because of the wreckage of a crashed plane a few hundred feet down). In bad weather, if you cannot see the wreckage, it is probably safer to continue east along the Niwot Ridge for just over a mile where a descent to Lake Isabelle to the north becomes a safer option.

Navajo Peak dominates the Navajo snowfield. To the right is the Apache Couloir

Apache Couloir

Steep snow, up to 45°
All day. Ice axe, crampons, rope and helmet required
A serious undertaking

Unlike the Navajo Snowfield which is open, the Apache Couloir feels steeper and more confined. An adventurous route to a rambling summit. The descent will involve descending steep snow down the Navajo Snowfield.

From Nederland drive north on Hwy. 72 to Ward. Just after the Ward turning, take the left to Brainard Lake. Follow this road around Brainard Lake to the Long Lake Trailhead.

From the trailhead, hike the Pawnee Pass Trail along the right hand side of Long Lake, and continue on past Lake Isabelle on its norther shore. The Pawnee Pass Trail turns right before the lake. Continue on west for the final 1½ miles of the hike, passing a small unnamed lake. The route is the most obvious narrow snow gully that lies to the left of the Apache Peak summit. It is about a 1,000' climb up to the ridge.

Once on the ridge, the summit of Apache is a couple of hundred feet away to the south.

From the ridge, hike south to overlook the Navajo Snowfield (easily identified by Dicker's Peck, an 80' high needle of rock). It is possible to downclimb keeping to the west. Or, some prefer to rappel about 60' to the col. From here, head diagonally down the lefthand side of the Navajo Snowfield to reach easier ground and the way home.

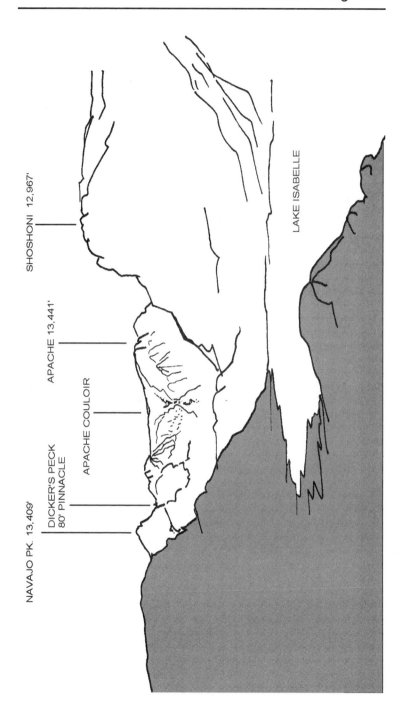

SHOSHONI 12,967'

APACHE 13,441'

APACHE COULOIR

DICKER'S PECK
80' PINNACLE

NAVAJO PK. 13,409'

LAKE ISABELLE

Shoshoni Couloirs

Steep snow, up to 45°
All day. Ice axe, crampons, rope and helmet required
A serious undertaking

The Shoshoni Couloirs are hidden gems rising from the remote Isabelle Glacier. They offer a snow and ice adventure well into the summer months.

From the trailhead, hike the Pawnee Pass Trail along the right hand side of Long Lake, and continue on past Lake Isabelle on its northern shore. The Pawnee Pass Trail turns right before the lake. Just past Lake Isabelle, zigzag up the hillside to the right, passing close to the waterfall (This is drainage from the Isabelle Glacier). From here it is a short steep hike up to the snow. We (the Authors) found hundreds of moths and other insects lying on the snow here, presumably carried aloft by the winds.

Wander over to the right to a choice of three couloirs. The right hand gully is on its own and doesn't stay in condition long after the winter meltdown. For this reason, the left two are probably the better choice. The far lefthand gully is more demanding than the central one due to the usual existence of a short rock pitch near the start. There is plenty of loose rock on this pitch. Otherwise both gullies are straightforward but may have small cornices which can be either tackled direct, or sidestepped.

From the top of the couloirs, the summit lies to the east, and the descent is to the north-east to gain the Pawnee Pass Trail. To get to the trail, you must descend a steep snowfield to the east. This can be descended direct, at a steep angle, or less steeply down the lefthand edge.

The western couloirs of Shoshoni viewed from the Niwot Ridge

Climbing the lefthand Shoshoni Couloir

East Face of Shoshoni

Steep rock climbing, 5.2 - 5.9
All day. Rope and helmet required
Serious - loose rock
Route finding is part of the difficulty of this climb

Dominating the valley, the East Face of Shoshoni is not often climbed, but is a fine outing for the experienced mountaineer.

From the trailhead, hike the Pawnee Pass Trail along the right hand side of Long Lake, and continue on past Lake Isabelle on its northern shore. The Pawnee Pass Trail turns right before the lake. Continue on west then leave the trail before the East Face and hike diagonally up to its base. Cross the lower slopes (often snow covered) to gain a series of undefined ramps. Avoid the right hand area of the East Face - this appears steep and difficult and probably is. Look for the line of least resistance. Near the top of the climb, trend rightwards to avoid chasms and tottering blocks (that look down into the Isabelle Glacier to the west).

From the high point on the buttress, it is a short hike to the true summit.

Descend northwards above a steep snowfield (which can be descended but may need the use of an ice axe) to join the Pawnee Pass Trail. This is then followed back east to the trailhead.

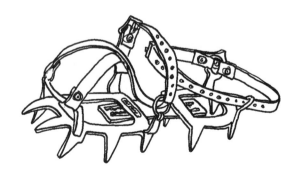

Shoshoni East Face, showing general line of route

Traverse of the Indian Peaks, Navajo, Apache & Shoshoni

Steep, loose rock with considerable exposure
All day. Ice axe, crampons, rope and helmet required
A serious undertaking

In July 1993, the authors along with Allan Tolhurst and Andy Blaylock set out at 3.00am from the Colorado University Mountain Research Station at the base of the Niwot Ridge. The object was to traverse the three peaks, Navajo, Apache and Shoshoni in a single day. Whilst the traverse is not a long trip in miles, it does involve complex route finding on a long, rugged ridge that forms the Continental Divide and joins the three peaks.

The Niwot Ridge Road is followed to the winter closure gate where the road becomes the Niwot Ridge Trail. This first section is long and tedious, especially so early in the morning. Past the gate, the terrain becomes more open with a tundra landscape. The Research Station is involved with a great deal of work in this area, and the fenced areas need to be avoided.

After about 4 hours the ridge is gained and the whole days route comes into view. A great place for breakfast and possibly a nap!

With the sun behind you head up the increasingly steep ridge towards Navajo Peak. Below and to the south lies the Boulder water catchment area which is out of bounds. Several false summits must be negotiated on this section which is longer than it appears. The lefthand side is probably the easiest. Finally the Navajo summit is reached.

The descent from Navajo to the west is fairly straightforward. There is a short steep chimney to downclimb which although only about 5.2 in grade, looks horrendous. The exposure on this section is quite fierce. Continuing down, the small col containing the prominent Dicker's Peak is reached. The Peak can be climbed at about 5.5 standard, although we passed it by.

The next section is a scramble up to the summit of Apache.

From Apache, the route descends down a way to gain an arete that form the next section. It becomes more serious from here due to complex route finding, loose rock and considerable exposure.

Should the route look too intimidating or time is running out, escape can be made east and right, down very steep snowslopes onto the Isabelle Glacier (an ice axe would be essential for this).

There are many options, none appearing too attractive. Often height must be lost to make progress along the ridge. Sometimes the best route takes highly unlikely ledges leading apparently nowhere.

Another large pinnacle is passed that is prominent from the glacier below. More shapely than Dickers Peck, we felt it deserved to have a name.

The traverse continues on in much the same vein. The Isabelle Glacier is obvious down to the right, but there is no easy escape from this section. It may be possible to descend to the west, but it would result in an extremely long hike to reach civilization (in this case Lake Granby).

Finally the ridge mellows out on the shoulder of Shoshoni and the tough stuff is over. An easy walk leads to the summit.

Descend northwards above a steep snowfield (which can be descended but may need the use of an ice axe) to join the Pawnee Pass Trail. This is then followed down and to the east to the Long Lake Trailhead. A vehicle left here the night before will help in returning to the Colorado University Mountain Research Station.

On the traverse of the Indian Peaks. Lake Isabelle in the distance

Reaching a control

Photo: Pat Albright

Orienteering

Also known as 'Cunning Running', Orienteering can be best described as following a prepared course using a map and compass to guide you.

A temporary course is set up with 'controls' which are marked with orange (or sometimes red) and white markers. The aim is to make your way around the course, locating the markers as you go. To prove that you have located the markers, you carry a card which is punched with a hole punch at each marker. As each punch has a unique pattern of pins, it's difficult to cheat!

A key skill is determining the best route between two control markers. You use natural features to assist in finding the marker as quickly as possible. The events are timed, so a certain degree of haste is in order, although one of the attractions of the sport is that it can be enjoyed by both young and old, families, and by people of all levels of fitness and competence.

The courses often cross a mix of terrain including forested areas, meadows and creeks. Hilly areas tend to be used more often than flatland. However, many cities in Europe have permanent orienteering courses set out in city parks.

Courses are usually graded using a color system which is common to the sport. Participants choose a course according to age and gender, or fitness. A typical meet will have a number of courses, perhaps sharing some of the controls, but giving very different levels of difficulty and length. One of the nice things about orienteering is that you can choose a level of difficulty according to your experience and fitness, and still have a good day out. As your fitness and ability improve, the further you can go.

Examples of the Courses are below.

Course Name	Length	Level
White	Up to 3km	Beginner
Yellow	3.5 - 4.5km	Adv. Beginner
Orange	4 - 5km	Intermediate
Green	4 - 5km	Short Advanced
Red	5 - 7km	Long Advanced
Score-O	Special Timed Event	
Rogaine	Special 24hr Event	

The meets are characterized by a very welcoming attitude towards new members or people who just want to try out the sport. All you need to compete is a compass (a protractor type is best), some old clothes as the routes often go through woodland and undergrowth, and a pair of sneakers or hiking boots.

There is usually an entry fee which helps cover the cost of the maps and other expenses.

As this is not really a sport that can be done on your own, the best way to try it is to get in touch with the Rocky Mountain Orienteering Club. See below for details.

Orienting your map

Photo: Pat Albright

Rocky Mountain Orienteering Club

A non-profit organization, founded in 1973. The club holds 15-20 meets per year, seasonally during the warmer months. Membership is open to everyone and includes a subscription to the club's newsletter.

For details, contact:

Anna & Michael Rounds	(303) 499-7371
Pat Albright	(303) 786-8502

Membership Fees 1993:

Individual	$12	
Family	$18	

Local Meet Costs:

	Member	Non-Member
Adult	$3	$5
Junior	$2	$3

Orienteering - a sport for all
Photo: Pat Albright

Paragliding at North Boulder, near Wonderland Lake

Paragliding

Paragliding is one of Boulder's more recent imports and is enjoyed by an ever growing number of enthusiasts. Imagine hiking up a hillside or mountainside then unfolding your paraglider (simply a high-tech parachute weighing about 15lb) on the ground. A quick tug on the control lines and almost instantaneously you have a flying machine literally at your finger tips. An upward glance at the paraglider to ensure all is well, and away you go. Relax back into your seat harness and enjoy the thrill. Initially your flights may be modest - just down to the foot of the hill, but with practice and experience, you can fly further and for longer. Here in this area, local records are being broken almost weekly, and 30 mile flights will soon be commonplace.

A common misconception is that the pilot JUMPS off the mountain. WRONG! Rather, the canopy is inflated into the wind by running down an incline. This is why the foothills are used. The speed of your run, combined with the head-on wind give the paraglider the airspeed it needs to lift the pilot up. In lighter winds, the pilot will need to run faster, in stronger winds, the run may be only a couple of steps. Once in the air, the sensation tends to be one of tranquility.

The best and safest introduction to the sport is through a recognized school. Most schools will take you for just a one day introduction course. Some schools offer tandem instruction, that is, where you fly with the instructor under the same canopy. Tandem flying is a great introduction to the sport and allows you to get airbourne much quicker. Also, because the pilot is very experienced, you will probably get a longer flight than would be normal on your first day of training.

Whilst a full Certification Training Course (Class One) is a multi-day learning experience, the average student should be flying short distances during his or her first day of paragliding. Class One Certification is the minimum requirement for flying at most registered sites across the country.

The sport of paragliding is administered by the US Hang Gliding Association (USHGA) based in Colorado Springs, which registers pilots and sets out policy for training and qualifications. Also, as the sport is recognized as aviation, it comes under Federal Aviation Authority (FAA) regulations and Rules of the Air.

Generally the sport is very safe, although as it is a form of aviation, it is important to take it seriously. We recommend that beginners approach an established school for flying instruction. See Reference 3 for schools.

The two major sites for paragliding in the area are North Boulder above Wonderland Lake, and Lookout Mountain in Golden.

Flying over Golden

Photo: Peter Kent

High over Boulder

by Todd Bibler

I have always wanted to soar like a bird. With a paraglider my dreams have come true. It is a magical experience every time I catch a thermal, spiralling upwards in the lifting air, sometimes all the way to the clouds. the quiet beauty from thousands of feet over the ground is hard to describe.

With knowledge and practice, flying cross-country becomes possible. I'll never forget my 6½ hour, 62 mile flight over the Canadian Rockies with nothing but air under my feet. Learning the skills required to achieve such a flight is the challenge. With a paragliders constant sink rate of 250 feet per minute, if you don't find and stay in air that is rising faster than your are sinking, your flight will soon end with a landing.

Boulder's front range is a perfect location for paragliding year round. Summertime lift is powerful and frequent, and winter up-slopes provide hours of gentle gliding. Flights of 20-30 miles are becoming common; such as my flight from Golden to Lyons, or Peter Kloepfer's flight from Golden to Rollinsville. Soon we will see flights from Boulder to the Continental Divide and Estes Park. Won't you join me?

Wonderland Lake and North Boulder taken during Todd Bibler's historic first flight from Golden to Lyons

Photo: Todd Bibler

Rafting Clear Creek Canyon
Photo: Clear Creek Rafting/Photo Maniacs

Rafting

In our research we found that most Boulderites are not aware that river rafting is possible within a one hour drive. The only river that is rafted commercially, to our knowledge, in this area is Clear Creek from above Idaho Springs down to Golden. The best season for river rafting on Clear Creek is mid-May to mid-August. The best (and therefore most popular) month is July, so booking ahead during this period may be a wise move. Bear in mind that the river can still be chilly in June and a paddle suit will make getting drenched less unpleasant. These are usually available from the tour operator.

Clear Creek's major characteristic is that the water flow is not controlled, but all natural. It is also not as crowded as some of the more popular rafting rivers in the state. During the spring runoff, Clear Creek becomes quite a sizable river with volumes up to 1,200 cubic feet per second, which if difficult to visualize, is certainly big enough for a thrill. Clear Creek is well endowed with rapids, perhaps more than any other commercially rafted river in the state. The rapids reach to Class III and IV on the section just before Idaho Springs. Below the town, the angle eases and the creek is more gentle until it passes under I-70. This section is popular with families and the faint of heart. From Idaho Springs down to Golden the creek reverts back to a more aggressive character. The tours usually run 2-3 hours in length.

The secret of success when negotiating a wild river is teamwork. The rabid isolationist may want to take up kayaking instead!

A list of some of the operators running the Creek is listed in Reference 3.

Reaching the pain barrier on the Old Stage Road
Photo: Anne Krause

Road Cycling

B oulder is one of the truly great meccas for cyclists in the United States. The town has a long tradition of cycling which gained a considerable boost by the organization of the Red Zinger Classic (which changed later into the Coors Classic) in the mid-1970's. The Classic was the premier american road race for many years and attracted riders from around the world.

The proximity of Boulder to the Colorado Springs Olympic Training Center has led to it being a popular base for many top level cyclists, and their presence has proved a draw for aspiring cyclists who want to train against the best.

Bike lanes are a help in getting around the town, but it is the ability to 'get out of town' quickly, coupled with the clean Rocky Mountain air that gives the pleasure of cruising those roadways available on every side of town. The high altitude, and its benefit to serious road and track training has, and will, continue to bring into the area the elite of the cycling world.

The abundance of training facilities, clubs, bicycle shops and all type of road grades make it possibly the most popular sport in town. There are reckoned to be more professional cyclists per capita in Boulder than any other town in the USA.

Some of the routes listed here may be a bit too much for the more casual rider due to their loop nature. They do offer some of amazing riding and are worth working up to.

For more information about cycling locally contact:
Boulder Velo Club at PO Box 17934, Boulder, CO. 80308
or visit one of the cycling stores in town.

Suggested Routes

Peak to Peak Highway

One of the great scenic roads in Colorado, the Peak to Peak Highway from Nederland to Estes is very popular. Start from Nederland and head north, as far as you want, and return. The road is hilly but there is a wide shoulder and the views and high altitude make up for it. It is possible to ride up to meet the highway from Boulder, but the canyons tend to be busy and narrow, and are really only for the very fit. Avoid at all costs cycling up Boulder Canyon to get to Nederland, it is an unpleasant experience.

Mt Evans

For the ultra fit, or merely masochistic, the ride up the highest paved road in the USA is a great challenge. Take I-70 west to Idaho Springs, exit and park at the U.S Forest Service station. The ride is 28 miles to the summit, starting at 7,000' and ending at 14,264 feet. The road is only open during the summer months and even then you should be ready for rain or snow showers. Scene of an annual race, this is a great ride for the adventurous.

Apple Valley Loop

Take Hwy. 36 north out of Boulder to the junction with Hwy. 66 outside Lyons. (The final 6 miles of Hwy. 36 has only a narrow shoulder so take care). At Hwy. 66, turn left and ride into Lyons. Take a right in town onto Hwy. 36 again towards Estes, then after ¼ mile, turn left onto the Old Apple Valley Road which is followed in a loop until it rejoins Hwy. 36. Back on Hwy. 36, turn right back towards Lyons. Follow Hwy. 66 out of the town and continue on it to the right turn for Hygiene - N. 75th - about 6 miles out of Lyons. Take N. 75th south all the way back to Diagonal Highway, which is then followed back into town. 35-40 miles. Rolling terrain.

The Plains Ride.

For a pleasant ride out on the plains with good shoulders and a great view of the mountains in good weather, this route is worth doing. Take Hwy. 36 north to the junction with Hwy. 66 outside Lyons. Turn right on Hwy. 66 and follow it to the I-25 Frontage Road. Follow the Frontage Road south to Hwy. 52, then take Hwy. 52 west to meet Diagonal, which is then followed back into Boulder.

Coal Creek Canyon

Start at the intersection of Hwy. 72 and Hwy. 93, just by Rocky Flats. RTD have a Park and Ride here. Follow Hwy. 72 west up into the mountains until you reach the Peak to Peak Highway. Turn around and enjoy the ride! 38 miles, allow 3-6 hours. Involves steep climbing but the traffic is not too heavy.

Lefthand Canyon to Ward

A beautiful scenic ride, but strenuous. Increasingly popular. Ride out of town on Hwy. 36 towards Lyons. After 6 miles turn left and head west up the canyon. At Ward, turn around and head back down.

Flagstaff Mountain

A strenuous hill climb above Boulder. Start from Chautauqua where there is parking and restrooms. The traffic on this switchback road can make it rather hair raising.

Mogul Bismark - Classic Race Course

Leave Hwy. 36 at the Superior exit and head south on McCaslin to the junction at Hwy. 128. Starting here, head west along 128 to Hwy. 93, then take it north to Marshall. Turn right on to Marshall Road and follow this to Hwy. 36. At the junction with Hwy. 36, head back along McCaslin to the start.

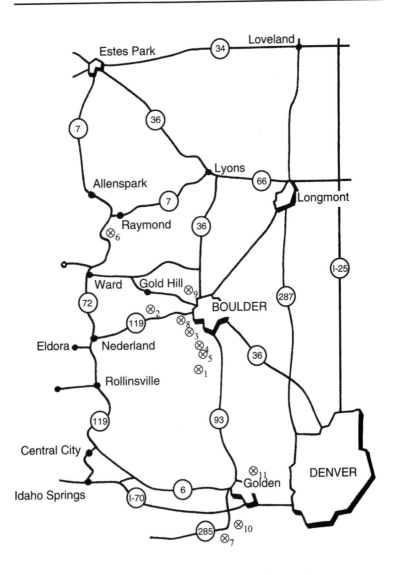

1. Eldorado Canyon State Park
2. Boulder Canyon
3. Flatirons
4. The Maiden
5. The Matron
6. Pete's Badille

7. Lovers Leap
8. Flagstaff Mountain
9: Mt. Sanitas
10: Morrison
11: North Table Top Mountain

Rock Climbing

As one of the world centers for rock climbing, Boulder needs little introduction. The sheer variety, quality and scope of the climbing in this area is enough to make climbers the world over green with envy. From the generally easy long routes on the Flatirons overlooking the town, to the hard test pieces at Eldorado Canyon and the recent sport climbs near Golden - they offer something for every climber. Throw in a bunch of superb bouldering areas and a handful of climbing gyms, and the result tells you why so many climbers from around the world choose to live here.

The great thing about the climbing in the Boulder area is that there is so much of it. If you seek peace and harmony in a mountain setting, no problem, and you don't even have to settle for mediocre climbs. The climbs at Eldorado Canyon and at Castle Rock in Boulder Canyon cater for those unwilling to walk too far. For that privilege however, you will probably share the crag with a host of others.

A word to the Neophyte.

Climbing is one of those sports where, for the inexperienced, it is ridiculously easy to get into difficulties without trying very hard. What may be easy to climb up initially may become too hard to continue, and worse, impossible to reverse. The numerous accidents at Boulder Falls pays testimony to the problems that the inexperienced can get into. To save yourself this embarrassment and possible injury/death, we strongly recommend trying the sport either through going to a rock gym or by getting some instruction from one of the local climbing schools. We have listed some of these in Reference 3.

Eldorado Canyon State Park

A valid State Park Pass is required for every vehicle entering the Park. Daily Pass for a vehicle is $3. Annual Pass $30.

To reach the Park, take Broadway south out of Boulder towards Golden on Hwy. 93. Take the Eldorado Springs turning 5 miles out of town, Hwy. 170. Drive through the town of Eldorado Springs, the entrance to the State Park being at the west end.

The Wind Tower

Park for the Wind Tower in the lot just inside the Park. Cross the creek by the footbridge to the base of the talus gully. The Wind Tower is up on the right from here, and offers two of the most popular routes in the Canyon, although the large amount of loose rock lying on ledges can make it exciting when parties are climbing above. Be careful!

1:    **CALYPSO**   5.6

Calypso starts from the lefthand side of the obvious block that leans against the face.

    1.1   From the block, gain the dihedral above by either traversing in from the left, or by climbing the chimney direct. Climb the dihedral, passing a small roof on the right and then up to a two bolt belay.

    1.2   The crack on the left above the belay is taken up to the walk-off ledge. Walk off to the left from the belay along the rotten ledge, or for a 'summit finish',

    1.3   From the belay, move dynamically directly up then go right and back left past a stunted tree to the top.

2:    **WIND RIDGE**   5.6

A justifiably popular route, the Wind Ridge follow the lefthand edge of the Wind Tower. Start from behind a tree on a ledge at the far left of the main face.

    2.1   Climb up the lefthand side of the arete initially for a short distance until it is possible to break right, over the arete, and gain the slab. Climb the slab up the middle to a large sloping belay ledge.

2.2   Using the obvious crack, continue up the center of the slab just to the right of the arete. Continue on up to belay on the walk-off ledge. Walk-off to the left along the ledge.

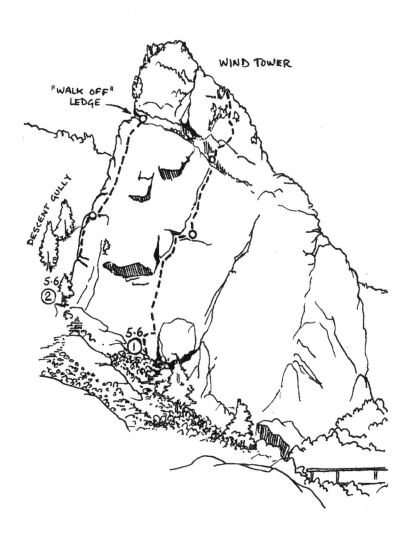

WIND TOWER

"WALK OFF" LEDGE

DESCENT GULLY

5.6
②

5.6
①

Redgarden Wall - South Buttress

Redgarden Wall is the enormous area of rock to the left of the Wind Tower. The South Buttress is the first section to be reached after crossing the creek by the bridge.

1:      **THE BULGE**   5.7
A great climb but take care with placing protection if the second is inexperienced, as there have been many 'incidents' on this route. Start from the ledge behind the Whale's Tail.

> 1.1   Climb the left-trending crack to a small overlap which is turned on the right. Continue up over a steep wall to a two bolt belay.
>
> 1.2   Go right for 20' using underclings to gain the ramp which is followed up and left to a bolt belay.
>
> 1.3   Climb right for a short distance then straight up for 20' to just to the right of a bolt. Traverse left to the bolt then go up and left for 60' to the belay stance.
>
> 1.4   Go right to join the descent path, which goes down to the gully on the right.

2:      **C'EST LA VIE**   5.11c
The first pitch is often done on its own - a fine 5.9 climb. Rappel from the belay bolts in the dihedral.

> 2.1   Climb straight up the wall, then layback the flake. There are chains under the roof to belay at, or you can continue left up over the roof and traverse left to the bolt belay in the dihedral.
>
> 2.2   Climb the dihedral with the crux about halfway up, then out right to a belay. Rappel 150' from here to the ground.

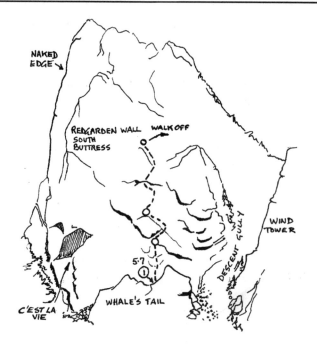

NAKED EDGE

REDGARDEN WALL SOUTH BUTTRESS

WALK OFF

WIND TOWER

DESCENT GULLY

5·7 ①

WHALE'S TAIL

C'EST LA VIE

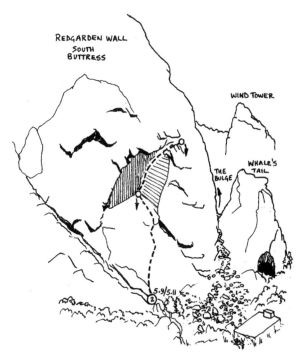

REDGARDEN WALL SOUTH BUTTRESS

WIND TOWER

THE BULGE

WHALE'S TAIL

5·9/5·11 ②

Redgarden Wall - Tower Two

Further round to the west lies Tower Two, characterized by an almost vertical clean knife edge that is the famous profile of the Naked Edge. The Naked Edge is probably the most famous climb in Colorado, and a magnificent outing. A fairly complex line, it is long and sustained.

1:      **TOUCH 'N' GO**   5.9

The original start to the Naked Edge, Touch 'n' Go is a fine climb in its own right. Start at the flake near where the trail from the river reaches the face, about 30' up from the riverside trail.

> 1.1   Climb up and left under a roof, over a overhang then up a crack to a sloping ledge (possible belay). Continue up and left to a right facing dihedral, ascend this to the large grassy ledge. Bolt belay. Rappel from here back down.

2:      **THE NAKED EDGE**   5.11a

> 2.1   Pitch 1 of Touch 'n' Go. Follow the grassy ledge up to the cave. Ascend to the stance above the cave.
> 2.2   Climb the finger crack to a bolt belay.
> 2.3   Go up the slab then left round the arete and up a short wall to a small ledge.
> 2.4   Continue up the arete, then step right and up to belay beneath a chimney.
> 2.5   Tackle the crack and corner, then go out right of the chimney to belay on the arete.
> 2.6   Moving up, pull around the arete to the east side and climb up the overhanging crack to belay on the right.
> 2.7   Go round the arete to the left and on easily to the top.

Descend by the slabs to the east, trending left into the gully that separates Redgarden Wall and the Wind Tower.

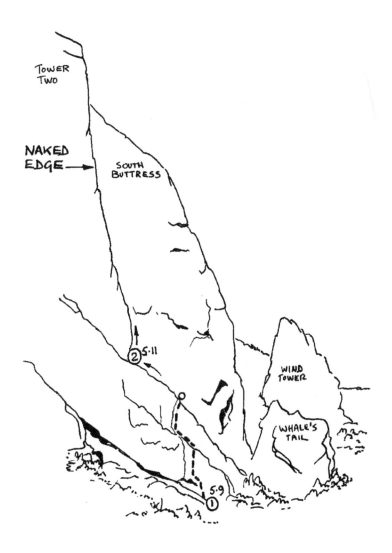

TOWER
TWO

NAKED
EDGE→

SOUTH
BUTTRESS

② 5·11

WIND
TOWER

WHALE'S
TAIL

① 5·9

Karin on the first pitch of Calypso. Note the sling placed to protect the second

The groove on Touch n' Go

Redgarden Wall - West Face

Redgarden Wall West Face contains numerous fine lines. To get to the face, continue round the bottom of Redgarden Wall and take the West Face Trail up the hillside. As you climb up, Lumpe Tower swings into view. Yellow Spur and the Swanson Arete start from just off the trail.

There is no easy descent from Redgarden Wall, particularly in the dark, so bear this in mind before setting out late in the afternoon. The most common descent is probably by rappelling from the notch between Tower One and the Lumpe Tower. There are two rappels down to the Red Ledge, then traverse across the bottom of Swanson Arete to the West Chimney. Rappel 150' down to the base of the chimney. It is also possible to walk off by the slabs on the east face, down to the descent gully between the Wind Tower and Redgarden Wall. It is however, a fairly complex route and not recommended in the dark, particularly if you are not familiar with it.

1:      **YELLOW SPUR**   5.9

Start from the ledge that runs down to the right from the West Chimney, about 40'.

1.1   Climb up to the roof and over its left edge then back right to the belay at a tree.

1.2   Go left into the dihedral, up this then belay on the left on a ledge.

1.3   Climb straight up to the large ledge.

1.4   Amble to the right and then ascend the large dihedral.

1.5   Go right, then up to a small belay in a spectacularly airy position on the arete.

1.6   Climb straight on up, then across left and up to a belay on a ledge, or straight up then right around the corner, up past a couple of bolts to the same ledge at about 5.10.

1.7   The arete leads to the top.

2:      **SWANSON ARETE**   5.5

Swanson Arete starts from the Red Ledge, a ledge cutting the face at about 100'. There are several options to get to the start. Probably the most popular is the first pitch of the West Chimney (5.6) which is not aesthetically pleasing and is also used as a rappel route. Alternatively, just to the left of the chimney is the vertical crack of Great Zot. This is a fine pitch at 5.8. Climb the crack into the small cave, then straight out over the cave lip and and on up to the Red Ledge. After belaying here, it is easier to move the belay right along the ledge to the tree at the start of the Swanson Arete.

2.1   From the highest point on the ledge, just behind a tree, climb the cracks up to another tree for a full rope length.

2.2   Continue up in similar style.

2.3   The real meat of the climb. Continue up, aiming for a clean dihedral beneath the Lumpe Tower. Get into the dihedral, then climb the crack with excellent finger jams to the tree. Go up and right through the gap in the final overhang. A fine pitch.

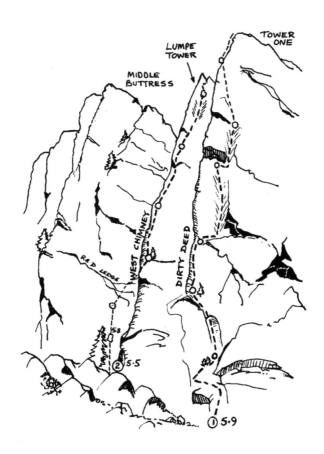

The Bastille

The Bastille, like the Wind Tower, is extremely popular due to its easy access and classic climbs.

Werk Supp and Bastille Crack start right from the road way (perfect for impressing the constant stream of visitors at weekends) and care should be taken for this reason.

From Werk Supp, descend down to the east, taking care with loose rock. To descend from Bastille Crack and Outer Space, work to the south of the summit via a series of ledges to get to the south side of the crag. Then pick your way carefully along the west side of the crag, keeping as close as possible to the base of the crag to reach the road.

1: **WERK SUPP**   5.9
Start 10' to the right of the blocky gully.
1.1   Climb up and over the bulge, then follow the crack straight up to the ledge.
1.2   Move the belay down to the left, below the obvious crack. Steam up the right leaning crack. Descend down to the left past the tree.

2: **BASTILLE CRACK**   5.7
Eldorado's roadside classic, with the perfect approach. The first two pitches can be climbed as one.
2.1   Jam the obvious crack to good bolt belay.
2.2   Continue in the same vein, to a sloping stance.
2.3   Ascend the thin crack to the large ledge.
2.4   Descend left then climb the gully which leads to the foot of the final easy pitch.
2.5   Climb the left side of the chimney to the top.

3: **OUTER SPACE**   5.10c
3.1   Pitch 1 of Bastille Crack.
3.2   Pitch 2 of Bastille Crack.
3.3   Traverse right for 30 feet, then climb the dihedral. Follow the ledge rightwards at the top to the belay.
3.4   Go left initially, then up the overhanging flakes. The route then zigzags to the top.

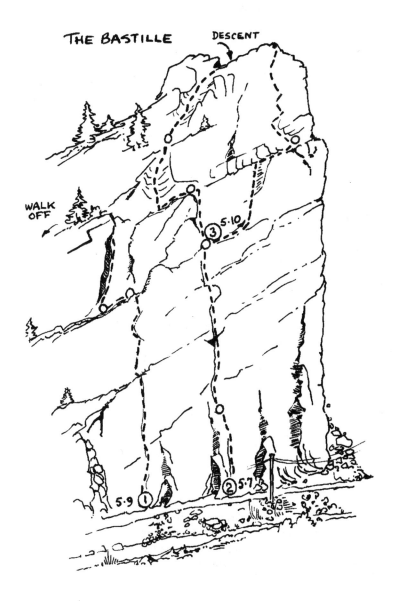

THE BASTILLE

DESCENT

WALK OFF

5.10 ③

5.9 ①

5.7 ②

Boulder Canyon

Boulder Canyon is 17 miles long and contains numerous granite crags, most of them minutes from the road.

The Dome

The Dome is located about a ½ mile west of Boulder on Hwy. 119. Just past the road cut, there are wide parking areas on both sides of the road. The approach is via the footbridge over the Creek. Take the path running back along the creek on the far side then strike up the hillside following a steep path.

The Owl starts just to the right of the lowest point of the crag. Cozyhang starts further to the right beneath several obvious overlaps. The East Slab starts further up the right side of the crag, just where the obvious crowd waits patiently.

The easiest descent from the top is down to the right.

1: **THE OWL**   5.7
   1.1   Variations are possible. Climb the easy ramp system up to the left, then head for the Umph Slot. Belay.
   1.2   Climb down to the right beneath the huge overhanging block, then up to the belay.
   1.3   Follow the ramp right to a final dihedral. Surmount this to the top.

2: **COZYHANG**   5.7
   2.1   Climb up and negotiate the overlaps to belay beneath the overhang.
   2.2   Climb down, reaching leftward for good holds. On up to the belay.
   2.3   Trend rightward and up to the dihedral, grunt over this, then easily on up to the top.

3: **EAST SLAB**   5.5
   3.1   Climb the corner to a stance below the slab. Either belay here, or ascend the slab above in one smooth pitch to the final roof. This is overcome by an undercling to the right.

THE DOME

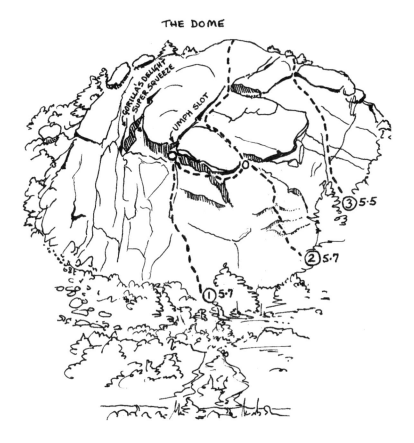

Cob Rock

Cob Rock lies about 7 miles up the Canyon, on the lefthand side. It is north facing and can be a rather cold and uninviting place except in the height of summer. Despite this, the crag has a very good line - Empor - which accounts for its popularity. Access to the Rock is complicated somewhat by the necessity of having to cross the creek. During the spring runoff, this may not be possible. There is sometimes a rope or long sling set up just upstream from the crag.

Empor follows the obvious dihedral lancing up the center of the crag.

1:      **EMPOR**   5.6

Starts just up to the right from the lowest point of the crag. Take the obvious weakness which leads up the left side of the fallen blocks.

1.1   Climb up onto the upper of the two fallen blocks.

1.2   From the belay, climb the crack just to the right of a corner to a sloping ledge. Tackle the main dihedral above. Belay at a small stance below the final steep crack.

1.3   Jam up the crack to the top. Escape can also be made from here by following the dihedral to the top.

Descend down to the right.

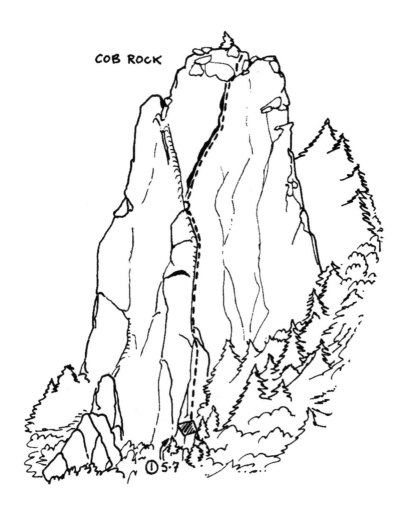

COB ROCK

① 5·7

Derek Hersey cruising on the South Buttress of Redgarden Wall
Photo: Beth Wald

Christina powering up the final pitch of Lovers Leap

Castle Rock

Lying about 12 miles up the canyon on the left, Castle Rock has the distinction of being highly accessible, with parking at its base and with the routes starting from just above the road. It is also a pleasant sunny spot, even in winter.

The normal walk off is via the North Face Route which is an easy downclimb. From the top, head north to follow a series of ledges down and round to the west.

1:      **JACKSON'S WALL**   5.6

A popular climb, with the final pitch proving the most testing. Start at the fire scarred chimney.

1.1   Climb the obvious trough to a small stance.

1.2   Continue up to a large ledge and belay.

1.3   Tackle the short headwall, then trend right to the summit.

3:      **SOUTH FACE**   5.9

Originally known as Jackson's Wall Direct. Start at the right facing dihedral.

1.1   Ascend the dihedral with a white scar, for about 30', then left to a ledge. Continue left for another 40' before climbing straight up to a ledge. Belay.

1.2   Go up for about 30' then delicately left up the steep wall to the belay. This is shared by Jackson's Wall route.

1.3   Follow the final pitch of Jackson's Wall, by ascending the bulge, trending left, then back right and up to the summit.

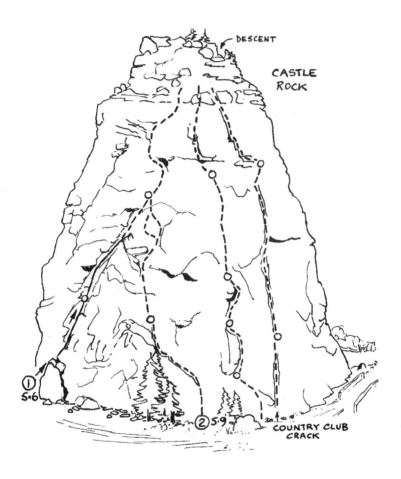

DESCENT

CASTLE
ROCK

① 5·6

② 5·9

COUNTRY CLUB
CRACK

FIRST
FLATIRON

① 5·6

The Flatirons
First Flatiron

The approach is from Chautauqua Park. Park at the Ranger Cottage then hike up the Bluebell Road to the Bluebell Shelter. Take the Bluebell-Baird Trail for a short distance to the north, into the trees. At the junction with the Bluebell Mesa Trail, take a left and head uphill. The trail is signed.

To descend, rappel down the southwest face for 100', or two 50' rappels - there is an eyebolt half way.

1: **EAST FACE DIRECT** 5.6

A very long climb, so long in fact that tedious route description will be avoided here. Starting at the lowest point, a smooth slab is the first obstacle. Then continue on up, trending left to reach the Arete after a few pitches. Follow the arete as it bounds exuberantly to the top. There are about 7 pitches, and, due to a lack of suitable anchors, it is not an easy route to descend if caught out by the weather.

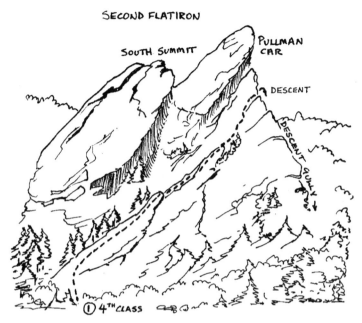

SECOND FLATIRON

SOUTH SUMMIT

PULLMAN CAR

DESCENT

DESCENT GULLY

① 4TH CLASS

Second Flatiron

The approach is from Chautauqua Park. Park at the Ranger Cottage then hike up the Bluebell Road to the Bluebell Shelter. Take the Bluebell-Baird Trail for s short distance to the north, into the trees. At the junction with the Bluebell Mesa Trail, take a left and head uphill. The trail is signed.

To descend, climb down to the north west for a short distance (very easy). Then follow the descent gully back down to the trail.

1:      **FREEWAY**   5.0

Whilst not difficult by any means, Freeway is great fun. The route is some 800' long, and individual adventurism is the name of the game. Beginning at the lowest point of the flatiron, climb more or less straight up for some distance, to gain the ridge. This is followed rightward to a notch which is best overcome by taking a leap onto the slab below. Catch your breath, then ramble on up gaining the northern boundary of the flatiron. The ground is tantalizingly close but inaccessible. One more pitch should take you to an easy exit off to the west. If you really must bag the summit, hike upwards underneath the Pullman Car - fancy name for a summit block - and climb the short West Face route at about 5.2 standard. This is also your descent route from the top.

Third Flatiron

The approach is from Chautauqua Park. Park at the Ranger Cottage then hike up the Bluebell Road to the Bluebell Shelter. There is a sign here for the approach trail to the Third Flatiron.

One of the most popular climbs in the area at this standard, it should not be taken too lightly as the descent is a serious undertaking. Double ropes can make the descent more pleasurable.

Descent: Take a rope as the only practical means of descent is by three rappels. The first is 40' down to the south - watch for arrows on the eye bolt - to gain a ledge. Another eye bolt shows the route of the second rappel of 50' down to Fridays Folly Ledge (take care not to continue below this ledge). There are two eye bolts here - the first requires a 140' rappel to reach the ground. The second - around the corner to the left (facing the rock) - is a rappel of only 70' down to the west.

1:     **EAST FACE**   5.4

Otherwise known as the Nike Route (Just Do It).

Hike up following the path until it reaches rock at a point about 500' up the right edge of the Flatiron.

1.1   Aiming up and to the left, amble across the trough to find an eyebolt to belay from.

1.2 - 1.5 Straight up more or less for another 4 pitches to the base of the deep groove that splits the upper face.

1.6   Drop down into the groove rightwards to gain the slab, then continue on up to a belay.

1.7   Continue up to the large comfy ledge known by some as 'Kiddy Kar Ledge'.

1.8   Walk along the ledge for about 10', then go up for 40' to gain the ridge which is followed to the top.

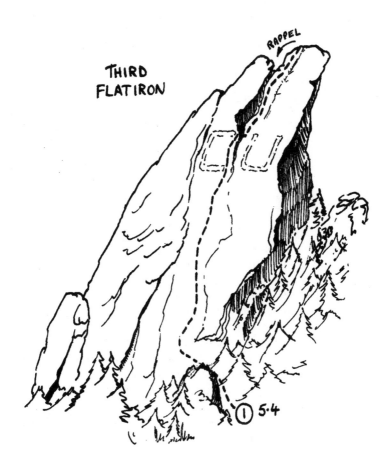

THIRD
FLATIRON

RAPPEL

① 5·4

The Maiden

Well known for its spectacular free rappel, the Maiden is a fine outing.

Park at the Mesa South Trailhead on the Eldorado Road - Hwy. 170. The old approach route was from the town of Eldorado itself, but the lack of parking makes this pretty much impossible now. From the trailhead, head northwest along the Mesa Trail to an old water tank. The Maiden is obvious from here. Head directly towards the Maiden up the gully and round to the north side to the far west end of the rock fin.

The descent involves a 115' rappel to a small ledge known as the Crow's Nest. It is then a further 100' or so rappel to the south to reach the ground.

1: **NORTH FACE** 5.6

Fifty percent down climbing, twenty-five percent traversing and, amazingly, the remainder is climbing. Despite this, a worthwhile expedition, with plenty of interest.

Not a good climb for the inexperienced unless belayed from both sides, such as in a rope of three.

1.1 From the base of the fin of rock, climb the short wall then belay halfway down the ridge.

1.2 Continue down to the notch - The Crow's Nest.

1.3 Edge down the north side then traverse to the obvious tree belay.

1.4 Work left to a large ledge.

1.5 Diagonally up (at last!) to gain a ledge which is followed down (for the last time) to a belay.

1.6 Onwards and upwards to the top.

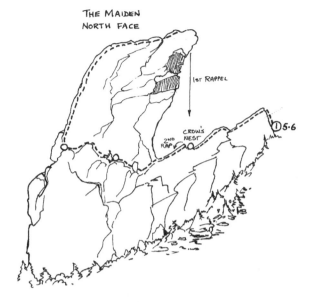

THE MAIDEN
NORTH FACE

1st RAPPEL

CROW'S NEST

2ND RAP

① 5·6

Hanging around the Maiden
Photo: Mark Springett

The Matron

Park at the Mesa South Trailhead on the Eldorado Springs Road - Hwy. 170. The old approach route was from the town of Eldorado itself, but the lack of parking makes this pretty much impossible now. From the trailhead, head northwest along the Towhee Trail to join the Mesa Trail. Continue west to the Shadow Canyon Trail and follow the short section of old road before cutting southwest up the hillside to the north side of the Matron.

To descend, rappel down the west face for two pitches - 60' to an eye bolt, then 100' west to the highest notch.

The North Face route starts from the top of a large block about 100 yards up the north face.

1:     **NORTH FACE**   5.6
1.1   Take the right hand crack up to the roof - ascend this on good holds then up to the tree ledge.
1.2   Climb up a 30' crack to the east ridge.
1.3 --   Follow the ridge to the top, the exact route is really up to you. Several pitches.

The thin crack on pitch 1 of the North Face of the Matron

THE MATRON
NORTH FACE

60'

140'

WALK DOWN

① 5·6

ASCENT GULLY

Pete's Badille

A little known gem, Pete's Badille does not receive the attention it deserves. As a result, the climbing has an exploratory feel about
it. A highly recommended route.

Located 7¼ miles north of Ward on Hwy.72. There is a large
parking area just before the crag.

The best descent is to amble down the gully on the east side
of the crag.

1:      **EAST RIDGE**   5.5

Start 200' above and round to the left from the lowest point of
the crag.

1.1   Slant rightward to an overlap at 50'. Traverse right
stepping down into a corner, and ascend a short slab to a
belay astride an arete.

1.2   Work back leftward to a ridge.

1.3   A full pitch of excellent ridge climbing to an obvious
platform passing memorabilia from the sixties (piton & ring
peg).

1.4   More of the same, sans memorabilia.

1.5   Slightly contrived. Deal with large loose looking
blocks, eventually breaking right to vault onto an easy angle
slab. Belay.

1.6   250' of alpine scrambling to the summit.

PETE'S BADILE

DESCENT VIA OBVIOUS 'V' GULLY

⑩
5·5

OBVIOUS "V" GULLY

Lovers Leap

Another crag which probably deserves more attention. It is located in the canyon west of Morrison on Hwy. 285. From Boulder take Hwy. 93 to Golden, continue south using US 40 to Morrison. At Morrison turn right and then left onto Hwy. 8. Follow this south to Hwy. 285. Turn right towards towards Conifer. Lovers Leap is the 450' high buttress on the left side of the highway, about 1 mile further on.

To approach the crag, drive past it then double back to the pull-off and parking area just below the crag.

Getting off is a rough and tumble affair down either side. The right hand side is probably the best.

1:   **LOVERS LEAP**   5.7

Start at the central section of the base of the crag, at a series of open grooves and corners.

> 1.1   Climb up and leftwards to gain the left facing corner system for a full ropes length to a small, well protected belay.
>
> 1.2   Continue up the steep, yet friendly corner. After about a half a rope length head diagonally left to a large cave. (If the belay bolt is chopped, continue above the cave for a more secure belay.)
>
> 1.3   The short steep crack above and to the right leads to a summit notch, an obvious feature from the parking area. The well protected crack is the crux of the route.

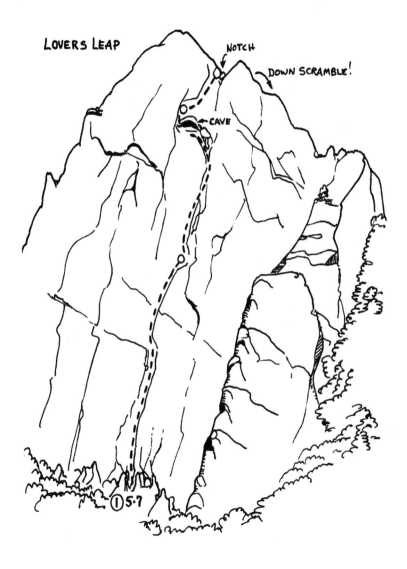

LOVERS LEAP

NOTCH

DOWN SCRAMBLE!

CAVE

① 5·7

Bouldering in the Boulder Area

Bouldering is climbing using the minimum of equipment on problems a few feet above the ground. A good bouldering area will have problems of all levels of difficulty. From a training point of view, the boulderer can work specifically on a particular type of climbing move as often as necessary. Boulder has many good bouldering areas, several of which are mentioned below.

Flagstaff Mountain

Probably the premier bouldering location in Boulder. Located close to town, the area is easy to reach although parking can be a problem. There are numerous locations in the woods, the further away you get from the road, the quieter it will become. New parking regulations require a parking pass if your car is not registered in Boulder. Tickets can be bought at Panorama Point on the mountain.

Mt. Sanitas

Not as heavily used as Flagstaff Mountain, Mt. Sanitas provides good sport, particularly if you wish to avoid the crowds. Park at the parking lot at the end of Mapleton Avenue just past the Mapleton Center on the right. The bouldering is located on the Mt. Sanitas trail which leads to the summit.

Eldorado Canyon

The Canyon offers numerous problems, some of the most popular being on the Whale's Tail down by the creek, and the Milton Boulder which stands by the side of the road about 200yds up from the Bastille.

Morrison

One of the hot spots for winter rock climbing in the Front Range. It is south facing so perfect all year round although perhaps a bit too warm in the height of summer. The rock is sandstone and very overhanging. Numerous bouldering and top-rope problems exist, and due to the over-hanging nature of the rock, it is a great place to build up strength and improve technique. Top-rope problems are 40' or more with wild swing potential and great bucket holds! A few anchor bolts have been placed on top of the crag. All in all, a great place, fun for all levels of ability.

Sport Climbing

Increasingly popular, several new areas have been developed in recent years which offer generally short, but hard routes.

For more detailed information on Sport Climbing in the area, check out '**1993 Boulder Sport Climber's Guide**' by Mark Rolofson.

One area that the authors have enjoyed climbing at, is described briefly below.

North Table Mountain, Golden.

A recently developed area, Table Mountain is south-facing and is a great place to climb during the winter months. Despite a rather scruffy outlook, the climbing is generally good and there are plenty of new bolts.

To prevent problems with access developing, please take care when parking - see diagram for the right place to park.

Due to the generally safe nature of sport climbing and the fact that the bolts will be obvious, we have not individually described any routes here. If a route looks interesting, try it - you can always move to another one if it's too hard.

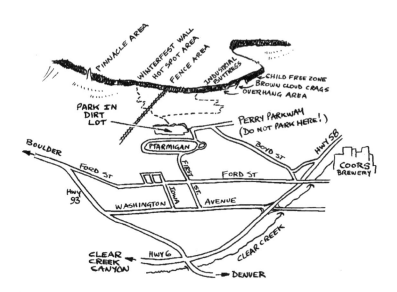

Mt. Sanitas the hard way

Running

Running is one of Boulder's premier sports. Just check out the facts and figures behind the Bolder Boulder 10km race that has taken place every Memorial Day since 1979. A total of 32,005 runners finished in 1993, a large proportion from the Boulder area.

Each year from April through September, the town swells in population as world class runners from all parts of the globe arrive in the town to train. Boulder has a great climate as well as all types of running surfaces. It has something to offer the recreational enthusiast right through to the elite runner, be it for track, road, trail or mountain running. There are perhaps not enough soft running surfaces - apparently these surfaces get blown away when the chinook pays the area a visit - but otherwise there is plenty of choice.

If you are new to the town, be aware that it usually takes about two weeks for the body to adjust to the altitude, regardless of your level of fitness. Many newcomers do not allow for this and push themselves too hard too soon.

The altitude of the town and the mountains to the west, offer easily accessible high altitude training. Runs such as the Magnolia Road and the Switzerland Trail, give 8,000+ feet of altitude within a 25 minute drive. The Brainard Lake area accesses an altitude of 10,000 feet within a 40 minute drive.

For the recreational runner, the gorgeous scenery can take the mind off the exertion. Do take care, on mountain roads in particular. Other road users may not be expecting you to be there, and certainly don't run in the middle of the road on sharp bends and blind spots.

The Bolder Boulder

The Bolder Boulder is the 2nd largest 10km and 3rd largest race of any kind in the US. Practically a Boulder institution, it is held on Memorial Day each year. The largest fully timed event, due to its wave start, it is also considered the best organized event. It has a unique finish at Folsom Field Stadium, home of Colorado University Football. The artificial turf within the stadium is a welcome relief for sore and tired legs and the atmosphere created by 30,000 finishers and their friends and families, is unforgettable. Even if you just want to walk the course, as many do, it is worth the early morning start. The race even has a year round information hotline line - (303) 444-RACE if you can't wait!

The course of the race has changed over the years, due in part to increasing numbers. The 1993 course is outlined below.

The authors in 1993 finished somewhat behind Arturo Barrios, but we are sure we could have gone faster if it had not been for the burden of research!

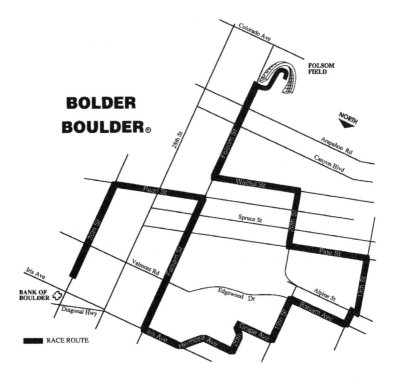

*The victorious entry into Folsom Field at the finish of
the Bolder Boulder*

Suggested Runs

Boulder Creek Path
If jostling with crowds is your kick, then this is your pick.

Boulder Reservoir
Favored by some of the best runners in the world. Its great qualities include a soft surface and minimal distractions (no stop signs here!).

Chautauqua Park
The Park offers a wide range of trails which can be joined according to you time schedule and stress level.

Flagstaff Mountain
A marvellous lung-buster, not for the faint of heart. Busy traffic and a narrow road make this an exciting proposition. There is, however, a well-signposted alternative path that leads to the top. This does, for the most part, avoid you having to tangle continuously with the cars.

Marshall Mesa and Community Ditch
A fine run on mainly level terrain. Park at the Marshall Mesa Trailhead and run west, across Hwy. 93, and on alongside the Community Ditch as far as the trailhead on the Eldorado Springs road.

Mesa Trail
The classic mountain trail. From Chautauqua Park to Eldorado Springs it is 6.2 miles. If you can arrange a ride back, then a dip in the pool at Eldorado Springs is a must.

Mt. Sanitas
A most enjoyable run with great views. The path is wide but stony and steep in places. A good training run for getting your legs in trim for the skiing season. The Mt. Sanitas valley makes a fine lunchtime run.

The trails in the other sections of this book will also make great runs as well. For the more adventurous runner, there are plenty of options, limited only by your imagination.

If you want company for your runs, here are two suggestions:

Boulder Road Runners Club
The club organizes a regular open run at 9am on Sundays at Broadway and Iris. Call (303) 499-2061 for details.

Hash House Harriers*

No piece on running would be complete without a mention of the Hash House Harriers (also known as 'drinkers with a running problem').

Began in Kuala Lumpur, Malaysia in 1938, by a group of British colonials drinking too much and needing exercise. Hashing is now very popular and has a worldwide following. The format is pretty simple. Runners set out to follow a 4 - 6 mile cross-country flour trail, en mass. The trail setters use loops and false trails to put off the runners, and this results in the runners having to adopt a team approach. When the trail is lost, runners spread out looking to pick it up again. When it is found, the cry goes out 'On, On' and the chase is rejoined. The finish is called the 'On-In' and at this point you are only halfway there! As its title, and unofficial sub-title suggest, this is not a serious running event, more a social gathering with a running theme.

For more information call:

Boulder (303) 494-5825
Denver (303) 526-0190

* Name comes from the nickname for Selangor Club Chambers dining room.

We went to great depths researching this book
Photo: Clyde Sole

Scuba Diving

Whilst it may not seem a natural scuba diving area, the sport is in fact thriving in the Front Range region. Perhaps it's because Coloradans are so far from warm water that they take their vacations in places like the Caribbean or Mexico, whilst others from out of state tend to come to Colorado to ski on their vacations. Who knows? Anyway, Boulder supports six scuba instruction centers and equipment suppliers, which suggests that it's pretty popular.

So where to dive?

To quote Scuba Joe (Joe Mottashed) - "The #1 diving location is Stapleton Airport. Just drive to Stapleton, and jump on a quick flight to the Caribbean." Thanks Joe.

For those unable to take his advice, there are several alternatives which don't involve getting to 30,000 feet.

The diving season in the Front Range runs approximately from late May through October. Water temperatures vary but at the surface they will range from the upper 50's in May and June to the low 70's in July and August. You will probably need a ¼" thick two piece wetsuit as well as the usual gear.

Of course, Certification is required, and you are strongly advised when diving at an unfamiliar location to seek an orientation dive from someone familiar with the area.

Local sites include Carter Reservoir, Chatfield Dam and Aurora Reservoir. For more information, check with the local dive centers. Phone numbers are in listed in Reference 3.

Back Country Air
From a Greg Anderson photo of Tony King at Yankee Doodle Lake

Skiing & Snowboarding

An immediate apology to those skiers who hate being lumped together with snowboarders and visa versa. We participate in, and enjoy both activities, and cannot see any reason these superb sports cannot co-exist on the same slopes.

Colorado and wintersports are pretty much synonymous. Skiing has been around in the state since it's very early days in the last century. Snowboarding made a significant local impact with the arrival in 1985 of the Snowboard World Cup at Breckenridge.

For both sports, a lesson for the first timer is highly recommended. Also, for skiers wanting to try snowboarding, be aware that its a whole new ball game - a lesson might well make the difference between continuing with the sport or giving it up after a frustrating hour or two.

From someone who has spent 20 years on skis and is still trying to feel comfortable in deep powder, Freddie couldn't believe how well he coped with two feet of new powder at Loveland after only a dozen times on a snowboard.

Lake Eldora (40 minutes) and Loveland (ok, just over the hour) are the two resorts featured here. Arapahoe Basin - our personal favorite - had, sadly, to be excluded due to being just too far past the hour.

During December through April, the backcountry ski areas may have full-on winter conditions. Gear up accordingly. April through July can often produce idyllic days of sunshine and long daylight hours.

Eldora Mountain Resort

Forget the hassles of driving on I-70, choose locally! Eldora's close location to Boulder makes it a great place to ski on a whim. You can even hop on the local RTD bus. Eldora offers great skiing, albeit on a smaller scale, and a relaxed attitude. The night skiing on Thursday through Saturday is a gas, and cheap to boot.

The snowboarding school is well run and surprisingly inexpensive. A one day lesson will include 2 hours of instruction followed by the rest of the day to practice your skills. It seems to us that there is a greater proportion of snowboarders at Eldora than at any other resort in the state. Far from being a reason for skiers to avoid the place, the relationship between the two groups is a good one. An additional good feature for snowboarders is that the resort has few flat spots, so it is easy to get around.

For the adventurous, there are also a number of 'secret areas' where one can find solitude and untracked powder (not that Eldora ever seems that crowded). Pro riders and skiers like Eldora because of the casual atmosphere where they can hang out. They feel more pressure at the mega resorts to perform well all the time. And this is really the secret of Eldora - it's a great little resort.

Directions: Head west out of Boulder up Boulder Canyon to Nederland. At Nederland, turn left and head south for a short distance to a right turn signed for Eldora Mountain Resort. Follow this road for about 1½ mile to a left turn which is taken up past a lake to the Resort.

Mountain Statistics:

Longest run: 2 miles   Snowmaking acres: 140
9 lifts including the new triple chair, Challenge.
Base elevation: 9,200'   Top elevation: 10,600'

Open Hours: 9am-4pm daily. Season runs through to mid-April.
Night skiing: 3pm-9pm thursday, Friday and Saturday 1/6/94-3/12/94.

Sample Lift Ticket Prices (1993/94 season)

Adult full day	$29
Adult Night Skiing	$15 (Valid 3pm-9.30pm)
Child (7-12) full day	$13
Child (6 and under with adult)	Free
Seniors (65-69)	$13
Seniors (70+)	Free

For more information call the resort on (303) 440-8700

Skiing the Corona Bowl at Eldora

Photo:Eldora/Tim Hancock

Loveland Ski Resort

Loveland has the advantage of being right beside I-70, just before the Eisenhower Tunnel. This makes it the quickest resort to get to from Denver. Beware of I-70 at the weekend which can seem more like a automobile rodeo than a major highway. Traditionally one of the earliest resorts to open each year, its high elevation often means more reliable snow than at some of the lower resorts. Like Eldora, it is not a huge resort, more a place to hang out and enjoy some great skiing or riding at a reasonable price.

Mountain Statistics:
Longest run: 1½ miles   Snowmaking acres: 150
10 lifts including one quad and two triple chairs.
Base elevation: 10,600'   Top elevation: 12,280'

Open Hours: 9am-4pm weekdays, 8.30am- 4pm weekends.
Season runs from mid-October through to May.

Sample Lift Ticket Prices (1993/94 season)

Adult full day	$32
Adult half day	$24
Child (6-12) full day	$13
Child (5 and under)	Free
Seniors (60-69)	$18
Seniors (70+)	Free

For more information call the resort on (303) 571-5580

Useful phone numbers
Colorado Ski Country USA has a number for ski conditions
(303) 831-7669
For road conditions call
(303) 639-1111

Loveland Pass

One of the best known free ski areas, Loveland Pass is ideal for car shuttling and offers the thrill of backcountry descents. There is the added luxury of knowing that you will not need to walk more than a few hundred yards all day! There is ample parking at the top of the pass on the east side. The views from here are continuously being captured on film by a never ending stream of tourists! Southward are Grizzly Peak and Lenawee Mountain which overlook the Arapahoe Basin Ski Resort.

First objective for the skier/snowboarder is the crossing of the road. Exercise caution as many drivers may be rubbernecking at the views at this point. You can start straight from the side of the road, or trek around to the west for a variety of ways down. Every which way will lead into the trees and magically you will be funnelled into the lower parking area, sometimes referred to as East Portal. Multiply 600 ft. of short and sweet descents by the number of times you can ride, car pool or hitchhike back up and you will have one hell of a day!

Steer clear of the finger gullies on the left as you come down. These are very prone to avalanche and carry a $300 fine if you get caught.

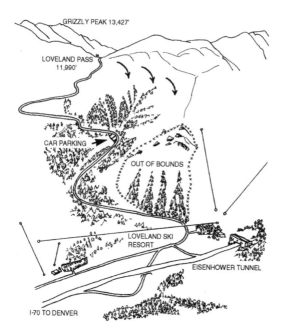

Rollins Pass & Yankee Doodle Lake

A springtime delight!

From Nederland, head south on Hwy. 72 to Rollinsville. Take the right on Forest Route 149 which leads to East Portal. Just before East Portal, take the rough road on the right which leads up the hillside. This is the Rollins Pass Road. The Lake is some 10 miles further on. Often in early season the road will be blocked with snow at a natural rocky gateway about 1 mile from the lake. Hike or mountain bike the rest of the way to some great snow slopes of over 800' in length. Just around the corner from the first obvious slope is Yankee Doodle Lake. Above the lake is a very steep slope with an hour-glass shape gully at half height. This slope should be treated with respect as it channels straight into the lake with possible dire consequences - swimming is often tricky with skis or snowboard attached.

These slopes can usually be worth a trip through to June or July.

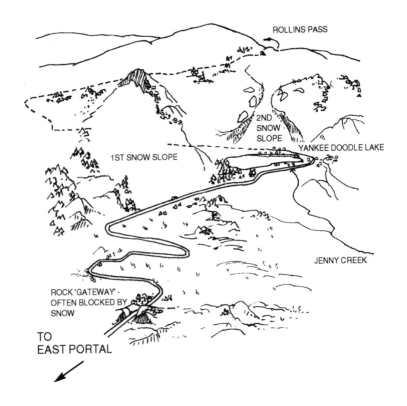

Telemark skiing at Yankee Doodle Lake in July

The Indian Peaks Wilderness Region

These runs offer an exhilarating experience. Springtime in the Rockies!

a)   4th of July Trailhead. Hike up towards Arapahoe Pass. On the right there are ample areas for skiing and snowboarding. These are on the southern flanks of South Arapahoe Peak.

b)   Navajo Snowfield. This is a very serious descent! Late in the season (usually around June) there can be much talus at the end of the run - don't fall into this area! For description and location, check the Mountaineering Section, page 184.

c)   Area to the right of Pawnee Pass. This is not in condition for too long. The runs are in a bowl to the south and below Pawnee and Little Pawnee Peaks. Rocky buttresses abound here and the couple of lakes may have only minimal ice coverage. In general - take care.

d)   The South gullies of Mount Audobon. These offer some challenging descents. Possible avalanche danger makes this a serious proposition.

Formation Jumping - a few formations

Skydiving

If flying at 120mph through the air appeals, then skydiving is a fantastic experience. The development of the square canopy has given the skydiver greater control, resulting in softer and more accurate landings. Such has been the progress the sport has made in recent years, that the emphasis has shifted to freefall flight.

Most schools offer three programs. The traditional static line jump can be completed in one day. After ground training, you will experience a 3,500' jump using a static line. The static line system is designed to open the canopy for you.

The Accelerated FreeFall Course (AFF) is designed for the 'true skydiver' and gives you a 45 second freefall from 10,000'. The course is one and a half days duration, with the jump on the second day. Two instructors will accompany you on this big occasion, their job being to ensure you pull the rip cord in the prescribed manner and prepare for landing in the correct manner. This course can form the start of a skydiving addiction and be considered part of your training.

The most popular course is the tandem freefall jump. With a tandem jump - where you fly with an instructor - you can be enjoying the thrill of a vertical mile of freefall after less than an hour's instruction. Great as a gift to an adrenaline junkie, it is also a fine introduction to the sport and can be accomplished in a matter of few hours.

Costs vary, but typically a tandem flight will run around $170. A two day skydiving course costs around $270. Some companies of observer rides - around $20 per person - so your family can watch your big moment.

Snowshoeing

Go into any of Boulder's outdoor equipment stores in early fall and check out the variety and volume of snowshoes hanging from the walls. By the end of the winter season nearly all will be gone. Several shops will have to re-order extra supplies in order to meet the demand.

Who buys all these snowshoes and what do they do with them?

Snowshoeing has become very popular and for good reason. One of the nice things about it is that it is an empowering sport for the less fit or older participants. You do not need to be particularly athletic, and unlike skiing, it is easy to get up after a fall. An added bonus is that they are lightweight - commonly running about 2-3lbs a pair. We have even heard that they are great for accompanying kids who are learning to cross-country ski.

We have used snowshoes here in the local hills, up in the Rockies stretching into Canada, and even on the Boulder Mall in the winter of 1983. We do not think it is necessary, however, to list any particular trails as being suitable for snowshoeing. Part of the fun is exploring trails and wilderness areas, and since the snowshoe has little or no impact on vegetation, it is possible to roam freely, snow coverage permitting.

Renting a pair of snowshoes is an ideal way to start, maybe even for a couple of outings. This allows you the luxury of sampling different styles, and when you are ready to buy, you will be able to make a more educated choice.

Snowshoeing in early winter

Just remember this maxim when contemplating your first purchase: there are no shortcuts. Invest $200 in a modern pair and they will last for a long time. Also be aware that there are different styles and that just buying a well-known brand, does not necessarily mean they will be the best pair for you.

Bindings are your main link to movement and mobility. Choose them carefully. Some manufacturers offer them already attached to the snowshoe, while others give you a choice of styles and functions. Most bindings have a universal fit, whilst others can be fitted with a neoprene sleeve to cover sneakers.

Everyone imagines the snowshoe runner cruising up mountains in wonderful style. But early snowshoe runners had to use designs unsuited to their running style: result - the front, or shovel, of the snowshoe would constantly bang them on the shins. Ouch!

Winter sports athlete, Bill Perkins of Leadville, Colorado, has contributed much to the sport in terms of research and development in helping to produce a worthy running snowshoe. Nederland is fast becoming a local hot spot for snowshoeing. Local guru of the sport, David Felkley, is a keen promoter of snowshoeing and leads tours around the area.

Clothing

As in all winter sports, layered clothing is the only way to have an enjoyable day out on snowshoes. Prepare for all kinds of weather, especially the cold. Gaiters are essential for keeping the snow out of your boots. Believe it or not, snowshoeing can be considered a 'wet' sport. This is because a fair amount of snow can be kicked up behind you. Some snowshoes are notorious for this action. Others are very well behaved, passive to the point of hardly disturbing the snow at all. Your shoeing style - be it brash, suave or stealth of foot - will contribute to you getting, or not getting, a wet back.

Footwear will depend upon the terrain you intend to cross, but sneakers are popular with the modern snowshoes, particularly if you intend to run or maintain a fast pace. Boots may suit those that suffer from cold feet, or if constant movement is not possible.

Ski poles are, in our opinion, essential. They help maintain balance, give extra push while going uphill, and also provide stability while going downhill. They can also help you get back up should you fall in deep powder.

Final Note.

If you don't have fun, then it's your own fault - snowshoeing really is a blast!

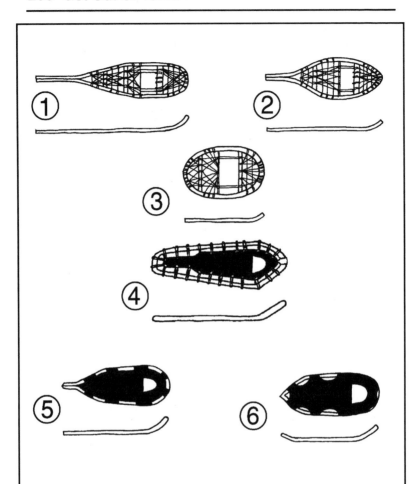

Styles of Snowshoes

1.   Yukon
2.   Beaver Tail
3.   Bear Paw
4.   Modern
5.   Modern Variant - Red Feather
6.   Modern Variant - Atlas Snowshoe

Snowshoe Types

Yukon

The traditional shape. Good for straightforward or long trails, as well as deep powder. The narrow shape makes it good for traversing steep hillsides and for descending. Heavier than other types, therefore more tiring on the feet. Suffers from poor maneuverability.

Beaver Tail

A popular and versatile shape, the flat toe makes it good for step kicking up steep slopes. The rounded sides however make it poor for traversing hillsides. The tail design gives very little drag when trailing in the snow.

Bear Paw

A short and wide design, with an almost flat bottom. The Bear Paw is good for kicking steps and has great maneuverability. A drawback is that the heel needs to be 'dug in' to prevent the toe from sinking too deep into the snow, which might result in a head plant!

Modern

Known by a variety of names including Western and Green Mountain. Basically a modified Bear Paw, having a smaller area, lighter weight, and turned up tail and toe. The binding is probably the most important part of your modern snowshoe (it's very often what you are paying for), and gives you precise control over movement. Smaller sizes are less suitable for deep powder conditions due to their having a smaller surface area.

Upskiing at Loveland Pass

Photo: John Prieto

Upskiing

Think what it would be like to ride the wind up to the high mountain peaks, then spend the day alpine skiing at 13,000 feet. The UpSki, which resembles a parachute, is used to cruise to the tops. On a windy day, a thousand vertical feet in a couple of minutes is normal.

In 1983 Phil Huff and John Stanford, two long time skiing and sky diving buddies, were back country skiing near Loveland Pass. Both appreciated the power of a conventional parachute on a windy day. Could such a device be used as mother nature's backcountry ski lift? After several years of testing, their quick venting sail system won a US Patent. Combined with a series of emergency releases, the UpSki today has maintained an exceptionally good safety record.

The equipment consists of a patented sail, control and harness system. The 15 pounds of gear, in a special pack, is carried to the base of a windward mountain side. Winds are generally from the west in the higher peaks of Colorado. The UpSkier unpacks the sail, slips into the harness and stows ski poles. The brightly colored sail snaps open and off you go! The views are spectacular, the speed and power are exhilarating.

Many expeditions have used the UpSki including the successful 1990 Norwegian Antarctica crossing, the American Women's Expedition (also Antarctica) and numerous Greenland crossings. Reinhold Messner, among others, has purchased 'off the shelf' UpSki canopies for serious expedition use. UpSkiers in Colorado are found mostly around the sport's birthplace in Summit County. UpSkiing is probably best known in the Scandinavia countries where several UpSki clubs hold inter-club races and events each winter.

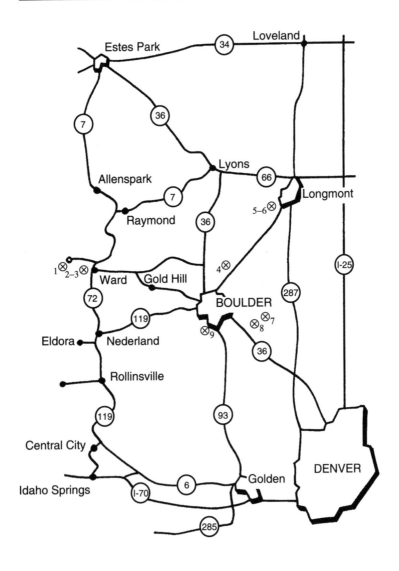

1.	Brainard Lake	6.	Fairgrounds Lake
2.	Left Hand Reservoir	7.	Waneka Lake
3.	Red Rock Lake	8.	Harper Lake
4.	Boulder Reservoir	9.	Viele Lake
5.	Lagerman Reservoir		

Water Sports

D espite its vast distance from the oceans, Boulder is blessed with easy access to a variety of lakes and reservoirs. If only for this reason, water sports enjoy a great deal of popularity. Add some wind to the equation (and Boulder has plenty of that!) and sail craft seem to appear from nowhere.

The Boulder Reservoir has a wide range of watercraft that are available for rental, these range from Hobiecats - an exciting catamaran dingy - to humble canoes.

If you wish to get involved in water skiing, Boulder Reservoir requires that all tow boats have a flagperson that watches the skier during their run. If they fall, the flagperson raises their flag. This is a signal to other boats to be aware that a skier is in the water. If you hang out near the jetty, it may be possible to offer your services - perhaps in return for a free ride.

The avid windsurfer may like to know that there is a telephone number that can be called to give temperatures, wind speed and direction for the previous hour at Boulder Reservoir. The number to call is (303) 581-9463.

In this section we have listed some of the main locations for water sports.

Boat Registration

The registration unit of the Division of Parks and Outdoor Recreation issues registrations for boats. Boats may be registered by mail at P.O. Box 231, Littleton, CO. 80160; or registrations may be purchased at 13787 S. Hwy 85, Littleton, telephone (303)795-5180.

Public boating lakes and reservoirs

Brainard Lake

Directions: From Nederland, take Hwy. 72 north to Ward. Just past Ward take the left turn sign posted for Brainard Lake. Follow this road for 4 miles to Brainard Lake.

Permitted boats: Wakeless electric motor boats, canoes, rafts, sailboats and paddle boats allowed. No fee required. Open sunrise to sunset.

For more information call the U.S. Forest Service, (303) 444-6600

Lefthand Reservoir

Directions: From Nederland, take Hwy. 72 north to Ward. Just past Ward take the left turn sign posted for Brainard Lake. Drive along here for 2 miles to the Red Rock Trailhead. The road to the Reservoir goes off to the left from here. Unsurfaced road, suitable for high clearance vehicles.

Permitted boats: Wakeless electric motor boats, canoes, rafts, sailboats and paddle boats allowed. No fee required. Open sunrise to sunset.

For more information call the U.S. Forest Service, (303) 444-6600

Red Rock Lake

Directions: From Nederland, take Hwy. 72 north to Ward. Just past Ward take the left turn sign posted for Brainard Lake. Follow this road for 2 miles to the Red Rock Trailhead. Red Rock Lake lies just to the west of the trailhead.

Permitted boats: Wakeless electric motor boats, canoes, rafts, sailboats and paddle boats allowed. No fee required. Open sunrise to sunset.

For more information call the U.S. Forest Service, (303) 444-6600

Boulder Reservoir

Directions: 2 miles north on Diagonal towards Longmont. Take a left at Jay, then take 51st almost immediately. Drive north on 51st for 1½ miles. Reservoir is off to the right.

Telephone numbers for information:

Beach (303) 441-3469   Boat Concession (303) 441-3456

Entry Gate (303) 441-3468   Main Office (303) 441-3461
Gate Fees : 1993 Season

Senior (65+)	Free
Senior (60-64yrs)	$1.50
Adult (19+)	$3.50
Teen (13-18)	$2.25
Child (6-12)	$1.50
Children (under 6)	Free

Season Permits available.

Sailing permitted daily - 6am to dusk.
Boat Rental Rates - (1993) Deposit & Driving License required.

Type	Hourly Rate
Mutineer 15	$20
Hobie 16	$20
Hobie 14	$15
Sailboard	$10
Motorboat 8 HP	$10
Sunfish	$9
Canoe	$5
Ripple Boats	$4
Row Boats	$4
Life Jackets	$3 per day

Lagerman Reservoir

Directions: 4 miles south-west of Longmont on Pike Rd.
Permitted boats: 7.5 hp or less motor, wakeless speedboats; no sailboats or sailboards. No fee is required. Open sunrise to sunset.
For more information call Boulder County Parks and Open Space, (303) 441-3950

Fairgrounds Lake

Directions: Hover & Rogers Roads in Longmont.
Permitted boats: Belly boats only.
No fee required. Open sunrise to sunset.
For more information call Boulder County Parks and Open Space, (303) 441-3950

Waneka Reservoir

Directions: 1600 Caria Drive in Lafayette.

Permitted boats: Concession boating only, with rowboat, paddle boats and canoes; no motor boats or sailboats. Open Memorial Day through Labor Day; Monday-Friday 3:00 p.m. to sunset; Saturday and Sunday 8:00 a.m. to sunset.

For more information telephone the City of Lafayette, (303) 665-9053

Harper Lake

Directions: N. McCaslin Blvd in West Louisville.

Permitted boats: Rowboats, canoes and paddle boats only; no motor boats or sailboats. $15 annual permit fee available at City Hall, 749 Main Street, Louisville.

For more information telephone the City of Louisville, (303) 666-8327

Viele Lake

Directions: Across from the South Boulder Recreation Center, 1360 Gillaspie Street, Boulder.

Permitted boats: Paddleboats and canoes.

Concession boats available during the summer months.

For more information call City of Boulder, (303) 441-3448

Windsurfing on Boulder Reservoir
Photo: Anne Krause

Torn between sports - 4th of July at Arapahoe Basin

Afterword

After months of work, apart from being exhausted and wondering how we so grossly underestimated the time this project would devour, we are glad it is finished.

The devoted 'Get Out Of Towner' may appreciate our dilemma of restricting our forays out in order to write about those very activities. We also faced the problem many guide book writers face, of writing about places that may be better left as an oasis of peace for a few select others to enjoy. In reality, there are always 'secret locations' and the real challenge is to find your own. Indeed, as locations seem to fall in and out of popularity, some may well be recycled. What a delightfully Boulder idea!

Finally, we welcome comments, suggestions or corrections to this book, and they can be directed to the Publishers address at the front of the book. We will acknowledge every communication.

Reference 1

Accommodation

We have listed here a selection of some of the accommodation in the Boulder area. Prices given are for the 1993 season, and are subject to change.

Arapahoe Lodge

Tel: (303) 449-7550

Rooms: 47   **Rates:** $50 - $81

Restaurant: N   **Swimming Pool:** Y

Breakfast Included: N   **Non-Smoking Rooms:** Y

Handicap Access: Y

Address: 2020 Arapahoe Ave, Boulder. CO. 80302

Best Western Boulder Inn

Tel: (303) 449-3800

Rooms: 95   **Rates:** $60 - $84

Restaurant: Y   **Swimming Pool:** Y

Breakfast Included: Y   **Non-Smoking Rooms:** Y

Handicap Access: N

Address: 770 28th St, Boulder. CO. 80303

Best Western Golden Buff Lodge

Tel: (303) 442-7450

Rooms: 112   **Rates:** $62 - $90
Restaurant: Y   **Swimming Pool:** Y
Breakfast Included: Y   **Non-Smoking Rooms:** Y
Handicap Access: N
Address: 1725 28th St, Boulder, CO. 80302

Boulder Mountain Lodge

Tel: (303) 444-0882

Rooms: 22   **Rates:** $35 - $85
Restaurant: N   **Swimming Pool:** N
Breakfast Included: N   **Non-Smoking Rooms:** N
Handicap Access: N
Address: 91 Four Mile Canyon Rd, Boulder, CO. 80302

The Boulder Victoria

Tel: (303) 938-1300

Rooms: 7   **Rates:** $89 - $179
Restaurant: N   **Swimming Pool:** N
Breakfast Included: Y   **Non-Smoking Rooms:** Y
Handicap Access: N
Address: 1305 Pine St, Boulder, CO. 80302

Briar Rose Bed & Breakfast

Tel: (303) 442-3007

Rooms: 9   **Rates:** $70 - $109
Restaurant: N   **Swimming Pool:** N
Breakfast Included: Y   **Non-Smoking Rooms:** Y
Handicap Access: N
Address: 2151 Arapahoe Ave, Boulder, CO. 80302

The Broker Inn

Tel: (303) 444-3330

Rooms: 116	**Rates:** $69 - $101
Restaurant: Y	**Swimming Pool:** Y
Breakfast Included: Y	**Non-Smoking Rooms:** Y
Handicap Access: N	

Address: 555 30th St, Boulder, CO. 80303

Clarion Harvest House Hotel

Tel: (303) 443-3850

Rooms: 269	**Rates:** $99 - $146
Restaurant: Y	**Swimming Pool:** Y
Breakfast Included: N	**Non-Smoking Rooms:** Y
Handicap Access: Y	

Address: 1345 28th St, Boulder, CO. 80302

Courtyard by Marriott

Tel: (303) 440-4700

Rooms: 147	**Rates:** $69 - $100
Restaurant: Y	**Swimming Pool:** Y
Breakfast Included: N	**Non-Smoking Rooms:** Y
Handicap Access: Y	

Address: 4710 Pearl East Circle, Boulder, CO 80301

Days Inn

Tel: (303) 499-4422

Rooms: 74	**Rates:** $59 - $69
Restaurant: N	**Swimming Pool:** Y
Breakfast Included: Y	**Non-Smoking Rooms:** Y
Handicap Access: Y	

Address: 5397 South Boulder Road, Boulder, CO 80303

Foot of the Mountain Motel

Tel: (303) 442-5688

Rooms: 18   **Rates:** $45 - $60

Restaurant: N   **Swimming Pool:** N

Breakfast Included: N   **Non-Smoking Rooms:** N

Handicap Access: N

Address: 200 Arapahoe Ave, Boulder, CO. 80302

Gunbarrel Guest House

Tel: (303) 530-1513

Rooms: 13   **Rates:** $72 - $130

Restaurant: N   **Swimming Pool:** N

Breakfast Included: Y   **Non-Smoking Rooms:** Y

Handicap Access: Y

Address: 6901 Lookout Road, Boulder, CO. 80301

Highlander Inn

Tel: (303) 443-7800

Rooms: 71   **Rates:** $53 - $86

Restaurant: N   **Swimming Pool:** Y

Breakfast Included: N   **Non-Smoking Rooms:** Y

Handicap Access: N

Address: 970 28th St, Boulder, CO. 80303

Holiday Inn Boulder

Tel: (303) 443-3322

Rooms: 165   **Rates:** $63 - $100

Restaurant: Y   **Swimming Pool:** Y

Breakfast Included: N   **Non-Smoking Rooms:** Y

Handicap Access: Y

Address: 800 28th St, Boulder, CO. 80303

Homewood Suites Hotel

Tel: (303) 499-9922
Rooms: 112   **Rates:** $101 - $131
Restaurant: N   **Swimming Pool:** Y
Breakfast Included: Y   **Non-Smoking Rooms:** Y
Handicap Access: Y
Address: 4950 Baseline Road, Boulder, CO. 80303

Hotel Boulderado

Tel: (303) 442-4344
Rooms: 160   **Rates:** $104 - $144
Restaurant: Y   **Swimming Pool:** N
Breakfast Included: N   **Non-Smoking Rooms:** Y
Handicap Access: Y
Address: 2115 13th St, Boulder, CO. 80302

Lazy-L-Motel

Tel: (303) 442-7525
Rooms: 53   **Rates:** $55 - $95
Restaurant: N   **Swimming Pool:** Y
Breakfast Included: N   **Non-Smoking Rooms:** Y
Handicap Access: Y
Address: 1000 28th St, Boulder, CO. 80303

Lodge at Nederland

Tel: (303) 258-9463 & 1-800-279-9463
Rooms: 23   **Rates:** $55 - $80
Restaurant: N   **Swimming Pool:** N
Breakfast Included: N   **Non-Smoking Rooms:** Y
Handicap Access: N
Address: 55 Lakeview Drive, Nederland, CO 80466

Magpie Inn
Tel: (303) 449-6528
Rooms: 5   **Rates:** $68 - $108
Restaurant: N   **Swimming Pool:** N
Breakfast Included: Y   **Non-Smoking Rooms:** Y
Handicap Access: N
Address: 1001 Spruce St, Boulder, CO. 80302

Pearl Street Inn
Tel: (303) 444-5584
Rooms: 7   **Rates:** $78 - $118
Restaurant: N   **Swimming Pool:** N
Breakfast Included: Y   **Non-Smoking Rooms:** Y
Handicap Access: N
Address: 1820 Pearl St, Boulder, CO. 80302

Residence Inn by Marriott
Tel: (303) 449-5545
Rooms: 128   **Rates:** $79 - $139
Restaurant: N   **Swimming Pool:** Y
Breakfast Included: Y   **Non-Smoking Rooms:** Y
Handicap Access: Y
Address: 3030 Center Green Dr, Boulder, CO. 80301

Sandy Point Inn
Tel: (303) 530-2939
Rooms: 29   **Rates:** $54 - $130
Restaurant: N   **Swimming Pool:** N
Breakfast Included: Y   **Non-Smoking Rooms:** Y
Handicap Access: Y
Address: 6485 Twin Lakes Rd, Boulder, CO. 80301

Silver Saddle Motel

Tel: (303) 442-8022

Rooms: 32   **Rates:** $30 - $100

Restaurant: N   **Swimming Pool:** N

Breakfast Included: N   **Non-Smoking Rooms:** N

Handicap Access: N

Address: 90 West Arapahoe Ave, Boulder, CO 80302

Skyland Motel

Tel: (303) 443-2650

Rooms: 51   **Rates:** $38 - $76

Restaurant: N   **Swimming Pool:** Y

Breakfast Included: N   **Non-Smoking Rooms:** Y

Handicap Access: Y

Address: 1100 28th St, Boulder, CO. 80303

University Inn

Tel: (303) 442-3830

Rooms: 38   **Rates:** $45 - $100

Restaurant: N   **Swimming Pool:** Y

Breakfast Included: Y   **Non-Smoking Rooms:** Y

Handicap Access: N

Address: 1632 Broadway, Boulder, CO. 80302

Reference 2

Equipment & Rental Shops

Boulder Army Store   (303) 442-7616
         1545 Pearl St, Boulder
         A wide range of outdoor equipment.

Boulder Outdoor Center   (303) 444-8420
         2510 47th St, Boulder
         Mainly water sports equipment.

Boulder Ski Deals   (303) 938-8799
         2404 Pearl St, Boulder
         One of Boulder's premier ski & snowboard shops.

Boulder Mountaineer   (303) 442-8355
         1335 Broadway, Boulder & Eldorado Springs
         Noted for rock climbing equipment & new routes.

Boulder Sports Recycler   (303) 786-9940
         1727 15th St, Boulder
         Good place to get gear - both new and used.

Chivers Sports   (303) 442-2493
         2000 30th St, Boulder
         Ski rental and sales.

Crank & Plank Sports   (303) 442-7265
         2716 North Broadway, Boulder
         Mountain biking and snowboarding specialists.

Duck Creek Sporting Goods   (303) 665-8845
    400 S.Boulder Rd, Lafayette
    Noted fishing equipment store.
E.M.S.   (303) 442-7566
    2550 Arapahoe Ave, Boulder
    Outdoor equipment.
Front Range Anglers   (303) 494-1375
    629-B S. Broadway, Boulder
    Friendly fishing equipment store.
Golden Wings   (303) 278-7181
    1103 Washington Ave, Golden
    Hang gliding & paragliding equipment.
High Peak Mountain Shop   (303) 258-7436
    1 W. 1st Street, Nederland
    Specialist climbing equipment and clothing.
Las Vegas Discount Golf & Tennis   (303) 440-4440
    1630 30th St, Boulder
    Golf equipment.
McGuckin Hardware   (303) 443-1822
    2525 Arapahoe, Boulder
    General outdoor and fishing gear.
Morgul Bismark Bicycles   (303) 447-1338
    1221 Pennsylvania Ave, Boulder
    Owned by professional riders. Bicycle rentals.
Mountain Mend   (303) 443-1925
    1833 Pearl St, Boulder
    Equipment repair and pack sales.
Mountain Sports   (303) 443-6770
    821 Pearl St, Boulder
    Snowshoeing and general mountain equipment.
Neptune Mountaineering   (303) 499-8866
    627 S. Broadway, Boulder
    Mountain equipment, speciality is ski mountaineering and
slide shows.
Firebird USA   (303) 440-0803
    4439 N. Broadway, Boulder
    Paragliders and paragliding equipment.
The North Face   (303) 499-1731
    Table Mesa, Boulder
    North Face retail outlet.

Play It Again Sports   (303) 499-2011
          653 S. Broadway, Boulder
          Good used equipment.
Pro Golf Discount   (303) 939-8555
          2525 Arapahoe Ave, Boulder
          Discount golf store.
Rocky Mountain Diving Center   (303) 449-8606
          1737 15th St, Boulder
          Diving equipment sales and instruction.
Runners Choice   (303) 449-8551
          1738 Pearl St, Boulder
          Running gear.
Runners Roost   (303) 443-9868
          1129 Pearl St, Boulder
          The premier running store in Boulder.
Scuba Joe Dive Center & Travel Agency   (303) 444-7234
          3156 28th St, Boulder
          Diving equipment sales and instruction. Also travel.
The Corral   (303) 443-0090
          1711 15th St, Boulder
          Horse tack store.
University Bicycles   (303) 444-4196
          9th & Pearl, Boulder
          Friendly bicycle store. Bicycle rentals.
Weaver's Dive Center   (303) 499-8500
          637-V S. Broadway, Boulder
          Diving equipment sales and instruction.

Reference 3

Schools, Tours and Instructors

Ballooning
      Aero-Cruise Adventures Ltd.   (303) 278-7181
      Air Boulder   (303) 442-5253
      Fairwinds   (303) 939-9323
Flying
      Dakota Ridge   (303) 444-1017
      Dan Guggenheim   (303) 939-9735
      Lonnie L. Hilkemeier   (303) 530-0550
Gliding
      The Cloud Base   (303) 530-2208
Hang Gliding
      Golden Wings Hang Gliding   (303) 278-7181
Horseback Riding
      Sundance Cafe, Lodge and Stables (303) 258-3426
      Lazy Ranch Riding Stables   (303) 499-4940
      Peaceful Valley Lodge & Guest Ranch
                        (303) 440-9632
Ice Climbing
      High Peaks Mountain Guides   (303) 258-7436
Kayaking
      Boulder Outdoor Center   (303) 444-8420

Mountaineering
     International Alpine School   (303) 494-4904
Paragliding
     Firebird/Alpine World Adventures (303) 440-0803
Rafting
     Boulder Outdoor Center   (303) 444-8420
     Clear Creek Rafting Co.   (303) 277-9900
     Impulse Rafting   (303) 567-4533
Rock Climbing
     Boulder Mountaineer Climbing School
          (303) 442-8355
     Boulder Rock School (Boulder Rock Club)
          (303) 447-2804
Scuba Diving
     Rocky Mountain Diving Center   (303) 449-8606
     Scuba Joe Dive Center and Travel Agency
          (303) 444-7234
     Weaver's Dive Center   (303) 499-8500
Skiing and Snowboarding
     Eldora Mountain Resort   (303) 440-8700
     Loveland Ski Resort   (303) 571-5580
Skydiving
     Rocky Mountain Skydive   (303) 430-1752
     Skydive Colorado   (303) 777-0225
Snow Shoeing
     David Felkley   (303) 258-3157
     The Lodge at Nederland   (303) 258-9463
     Mountain Sports   (303) 443-6770
Upskiing
     UpSki, Inc   (303) 468-8899 &
          (303) 468-8695

Reference 4

Recommended Reading

Avalanches

    The Avalanche Book   Betsy Armstrong
                                                           &Knox Williams

Cross-Country Skiing

    50 Colorado Ski Tours   Richard DuMais
    Peak to Peak Ski Trails of the Colorado Front Range
                                                       Harlan N. Barton

Fishing

    Colorado Angling Guide   Chuck Fothergill
                                                           & Bob Sterling
    Fishing Close to Home   Aquamaps

Gold Panning

    Gold Panning and Placering in Colorado. How and Where
                                                       Ben H. Barker Jr.

Hang Gliding

    Flying Conditions   Dennis Pagen

Horseback Riding

    Horsemans Trail Handbook   Jan Schafer
                                                            & Helen Eagan

Hiking

    Hiking Trails of the Boulder Mountains Parks and Plains
                                                       Vicci De Haan
    50 Front Range Hiking Trails   Richard DuMais

Mountaineering
      Colorado's Indian Peaks Wilderness Area   Gerry Roach
Mountain Biking
      Mountain Bike Map Boulder County
                        Published by Latitude 40° Inc
Orienteering
      Be Expert with Map and Compass   Bjorn Kjellstrom
      Orienteering Skills and Strategies   Ron Lowry
                                & Ken Sidney

Paragliding
      Walking on Air! - Paragliding Flight   Dennis Pagen
Rock Climbing
      Boulder Climbs South   Richard Rossiter
      Boulder Climbs North   Richard Rossiter
      Best of Boulder Climbs   Richard Rossiter
      Boulder Sport Climber's Guide   Mark Rolofson
      Colorado Front Range Bouldering   Bob Horan
      Flatiron Classics   Gerry Roach
Running
      The Runners Guide to Boulder County   Vici DeHann

INDEX

OTHER ADVENTURES

MAP

DESCRIPTION

OTHER ADVENTURES

MAP

DESCRIPTION

OTHER ADVENTURES

MAP

DESCRIPTION

OTHER ADVENTURES

MAP

DESCRIPTION

OTHER ADVENTURES

MAP

DESCRIPTION

OTHER ADVENTURES

MAP

DESCRIPTION

NOTES

NOTES

Further copies of this book may be ordered from the Publisher at the address below.
Price: $14.95 + $2.00 Shipping.

Please make checks payable to:
All Points Publishing, Inc.

Mail to: All Points Publishing, Inc.
PO Box 4832, Boulder, CO. 80306